Stray-Aways

Edith Somerville

Printing Statement:

Due to the very old age and scarcity of this book, many of the pages may be hard to read due to the blurring of the original text, possible missing pages, missing text, dark backgrounds and other issues beyond our control.

Because this is such an important and rare work, we believe it is best to reproduce this book regardless of its original condition.

Thank you for your understanding.

STRAY-AWAYS

BY

E. Œ. SOMERVILLE AND MARTIN ROSS

AUTHORS OF
"THE REAL CHARLOTTE," "SOME EXPERIENCES OF AN IRISH R.M.,"
"IN MR. KNOX'S COUNTRY," "IRISH MEMORIES,"
"MOUNT MUSIC," ETC.

WITH THIRTY-FOUR
ILLUSTRATIONS BY E. Œ. SOMERVILLE

LONGMANS, GREEN AND CO.
39 PATERNOSTER ROW, LONDON
FOURTH AVENUE AND 30TH STREET, NEW YORK
BOMBAY, CALCUTTA AND MADRAS
1920

AT THE RIVER'S EDGE

CONTENTS

LIST OF ILLUSTRATIONS

STRAY-AWAYS

IN EXPLANATION

WE have been assured on sufficiently high authority that the daily round and the common task furnish as much as we ought to ask. The question inevitably arises, why should we not ask for more if we want it? Personally, the thought of a stereotyped daily round is abhorrent, and nothing is less inspiring than a common task.

These sketches and studies represent the joyful moments of revolt of two working women, moments when wandering voices whispered editorially in their ear, beguiling them, like the distant call of the horn to the ploughman, to leave the long furrow, and to pull the horse out of the plough, and to ride a bit of a gallop over country of which, more often than not, they knew only that the going was deep and the fences blind.

But these excursions had for them the attraction, imperious to an Irish mind, of being any one else's work more suitably than theirs. Is there, for example, any Irish man or woman who could resist accepting an offer to make a harangue on Ireland, her politics, or her people? Or who, their normal task being fiction, could fail to find allurement in laying down the law in matters of fact? Let any one attempt to disintegrate and recreate fact as fiction and see if

B

it is not more entertaining to reverse the process, and, assembling one's vagrant memories on whatever subject may be suggested, to present what unsympathetic people might hint was fiction, as fact?

This last reflection does not, I make haste to explain, apply to this casual collection of by-products. Whatever merit they may possess is due to their candour, and to the fact that each represents an impulse, yielded to without resistance, an inspiring interval of escape from the duty of the moment.

I have attempted no classification of these recaptured Stray-aways. Many of them had strayed almost out of my recollection; Martin Ross's two earliest essays, " A Delegate of the National League," and "Cheops in Connemara," had, indeed, wandered so far afield that only after sedulous search in that ultimate fold, the British Museum, were they shepherded home. Of her two stories, one of them, "Two Sunday Afternoons," is now printed for the first time. It was suggested to her by what she had seen and heard in Dublin, when little more than a child, during the dark time of conspiracy of "The Invincibles"; and when she had written it, it seemed to her too sordid and too tragic, and she put it away and gave up the intention of publishing it. In this volume, however, I have wished to include all of her writings that are not already printed in one or other of our books, and, with but one or two exceptions, of work begun, but left perforce unfinished, I believe I have succeeded. I have, as far as is possible in joint work so closely interwoven as ours, indicated those articles for which we were individually responsible, and I have in some cases been able to give the dates of their original publication.

Of the chapters that describe our wanderings " In the State of Denmark," it may be said that they are written as it were from the point of view of Martin Ross (who did, in fact, write the larger share of them), and the curious in such matters may, should they so desire, compare them with other of her writings that I have reprinted here, and may, perhaps, discern something of her individual outlook in many of them. For the rest, they are now nearly old enough to be of value in throwing some light upon the manners and customs of ancient Scandinavia, and as such, may, I trust, command a small measure of respectful interest.

E. Œ. S.

1920.

AT THE RIVER'S EDGE

It happened to me to spend a winter night in the company of Anastasia.

It was in a village on the border of Connemara; we sat by the fire, and talked intermittently during our spell of watching. I did not wholly care for Anastasia, but she was companionable, and her interest in others was so abounding that it often overflowed as sympathy; that she was at all times a sympathetic talker went without saying. In the West of Ireland that is so ordinary a matter as not to be noticeable, until some withering experiences in other lands place it in its proper light. She was, of course, an Irish speaker by nature and by practice, but her English was fluent, and was set to the leisurely chant of West Galway; in time of need it could serve her purpose like slings and arrows. In all her sixty years she had never been beyond the town of Galway, and she was illiterate, two potent factors in her agreeability.

Everything about her was clumsy, except her large, watchful grey eyes; I have never seen a cow seat itself in an armchair, but I imagine that it would do so in the manner of Anastasia. She smoothed her clean blue apron over a skirt that was less clean than it, and continued to drop a few pebbles of talk into the dark pool of the midnight. Like pebbles they sank, and the midnight took them greedily into its deeps, because they were concerned with spiritual things.

4

" I wouldn't believe in fairies meself, but as for thim Connemara people, they'd believe anything."

Nothing was more certain than that Anastasia did believe in fairies, but it would have been impolite on my part to traverse a statement made to suit the standard of an auditor who could read books, and had travelled beyond Galway town.

" Out where me mother's people live, there's a big rock near the sea, and they say the fairies has a house inside in it. They have some owld talk that ye'd hear the children crying when the fairies does be bringing them in it."

Anastasia blew a sigh through her broad nostrils, vaguely religious, compassionate for the darkness of the Connemara people; to exhibit freely the devoutness which she indeed possessed was a gift bestowed upon her by nature. I asked her what she thought about the origin of the fairies.

" It's what they say, the fairies was the fallen angels; and when they were threw out of Heaven, they asked might they stay on the earth, and they got leave. 'Tis best for me go stir the grool."

In the silence that followed, while the gruel was being stirred, the low yet eager voice of the river outside made itself heard. The hazy full moon stared upon the water, and the water answered with glitter and with swirl, as it fled through the trance of the January night. The Galway river races under its bridges like a pack of white hounds; this little river, its blood relation, runs like a troop of playing children.

" But there's quare things do happen," resumed Anastasia, sitting down again with the caution that comes of perfect acquaintance with three-legged stools and four-legged stools on hilly mud floors. " There was a woman near me own village, and she seen me one Sunday evening coming over the road, and a bag of turf on me back, and she said I stood up agin' a big white rock that's in it, as I'd be resting the bag on the rock. Sure not a bit of me was next or nigh the place. But not a bit in the world happened me afther it, thanks be to God."

Anastasia sighed, in modest acceptance of her favoured position.

"It wasn't only two days afther that agin, there was a man from the same village seen me the same way. He thought to go over to a place he had his cattle, to look at them, and he said when he was starting out he seen meself coming over the road, and a bag of turf on me back, and he turned back; sure he knew I'd tell him how was the cattle."

The man was confident in Anastasia, as he would have been in any other woman of his acquaintance : he knew that she would look at his cattle as she passed, and that she would also be able to tell him how they were; this was a matter of course in their lives.

"Sure, I wasn't in the place at all, but whatever was in it, the Lord save us, he seen the woman, and he knew well it was meself, and she coming to him, and she in a valley, and it was the fall of the evening, in harvest-time."

Her heavy face had not changed, and the rhythm of her quiet speech had neither hastened nor slackened, yet the reaped fields and the dusk must have been before her eyes, must have seemed inevitable to the story. Better than "dusk" or "twilight," or any other motionless word, was "the fall of the evening" —the dew was in it, and the gentleness, and the folding of wings. There was that in the diction that summoned suddenly to mind the Shunamite, and the child who went out with his father to the reapers. Anastasia had never, I felt sure, heard of the Shunamitish woman, yet, had I read the story to her, she would instantly have understood that strong heart, and its pride and grief and rapture. Human nature was as clear to her as to the other illiterate people of her village and countryside, and, like them, she had the scriptural method of narrative, that curves on its way like running water, and sinks to its one and inevitable channel. I bethought me of the theory that the original Irish race, or some constituent of it, came from a southern shore of the Mediterranean; and all the while the boots of Anastasia confronted me, planted at the edge of the turf ashes on the hearth, like boulders on a foamy beach.

" But that woman that seen me the first time," she resumed, " she was a little strange that way in her mind, and when she came to live inside here in the town they said she drew a great many of Thim Things round the place. You'd hear them walking round the doors at night. Well, there's many a quare thing like that, and ye wouldn't know——"

The narrative faded out in murmurs that seemed to be both apologetic and religious, intended, I think, to present a proper diplomatic attitude towards all the powers of darkness. Anastasia lived by herself outside the village, in a crooked cabin with a broken door; she did well to recognise officially the existence of Thim Things. Her brother, over whose establishment she had once reigned, had married, and his wife was not favourable to Anastasia; that she herself had not married was an unusual state of affairs, but it implied no slur upon her attractions, nor did it imply the blighted love affair. Marriage, not flirtation, is the concern of Anastasia's social circle; the creature that we indulgently and sympathetically term Passion is by them flogged to kennel under another name.

Looking at Anastasia, I remembered a summer evening when I went to a Mission Service in a whitewashed chapel, and saw the burly Mission Priest standing before the Altar in his soutane, with the biretta forming an uncompromising summit to a square and threatening countenance of the bulldog type. The seatless floor of the chapel was covered with kneeling women and girls, in dun-coloured shawls or fashionable hats; the men stood at the back and along the walls, where the reds and blues of the Stations of the Cross flared forth their story. Even in their crude presentment of anguish, they seemed to say, " It is sown in weakness," but the oratory of the Missioner was a thunderstorm above them. Young men and young women were not to walk together in woods, or lanes, or after nightfall; the matter was made very clear, and was illustrated with stories appropriate to it. The audience was eager in the up-take, pliant and sensitive to every grade of thunder.

" I knew a most respectable young man," narrated the Missioner, " and his wife, a decent young girl; they had a nice young family." The congregation laughed delightedly and sympathetically, and the Missioner glowered upon them. This was not going to be a laughing matter. Soon there was drink in it, and a Protestant somewhere, I think; worse things followed. " The two of them are burning together in the flames of Purgatory," concluded the Missioner, with ferocity, and rumbled at them like an angry bull. The women swayed and groaned in horror, and ejaculated prayers.

I saw the congregation go home in the dusk, the women walking in parties by themselves, the men silently passing the public-house as if it had *Dhroch hool*, which means the Evil Eye.

"There was a Priest that was a relation of me own," continued Anastasia, rising to the surface of her thoughts again, in the manner that always suggested the rhythmic reappearance of a porpoise in a summer swell, "and he was telling me of a woman out near his own place, and she had a daughter that married and lived with her in the house, herself and the husband, and she got great annoyance with them, and they took the land from her. 'Well,' says she to the husband, 'when I die I'll rise out of the grave to punish you for what ye done;' and it wasn't long after till she died. I dare say they had too much whisky taken, and maybe they didn't bury her the right way: ye wouldn't know, indeed, but in any case the Priest went taking a walk for himself shortly after, and he went around the grave-yard, the way he'd have a quiet place to be reading his exercises. Whatever he seen in it he wouldn't all out say, but 'I seen plenty,' says he, and sure the coffin was there, and it above the ground, and no doubt at all but he seen plenty besides that. The man then that married the daughter went out, and he buried the coffin, and he got a pain in his finger, and he burying it, and the pain didn't leave him till he died in the course of a few weeks. The daughter was in a bad way too, after he dying; sure she got fits, and she had them always till she went to a sus-pinded Priest that lived behind Galway, and he cured her. Sure thim has the power of God, whether they're suspinded or no."

I asked her presently if she had heard of a Priest, renowned for his preaching, who had lived in the village forty years before.

"I did, to be sure, though I wasn't only a young little girl the same time. He was a great Priest, and after he died, it's what the people said, he went

through **Purgatory** like a flash o' lightning; there
wasn't a singe on him. Often me mother told me
about a sermon he preached, and I'd remember of a
piece of it, and the way you'd say it in English was
' Oh, black seas of Eternity, without top nor bottom,
beginning nor end, bay, brink, nor shore, how can
any one look into your depths and neglect the salvation
of his soul ? ' "

The translation came forth easily, with the lilt of
metre and the cadence of melancholy. Anastasia
looked into the fire and said, after a pause, " 'Twas
thrue for him."

I asked her what she thought of the Irish that was
being taught now.

" Musha, I wouldn't hardly know what they'd be
saying; and there's an old man that has great Irish—
a wayfaring man that does be going the roads—and
he says to me, ' Till yestherday comes again,' says he,
' the Irish that they're teaching now will never be
like the old Irish.' The Irish were deep-spoken
people long ago," continued Anastasia, yawning lamentably; " it was all love-songs they had. The people used
to be in love then. Sure, there's no talk of love now."

She said it comfortably, and presently dozed, and
I wondered what talk of love she had heard. With
the large eyelids closed, her face gained in tranquillity,
because the grey eyes were not truly tranquil, they
were only slow, with side-glances that revealed a
disposition both ruminative and quick. It was not
easy to imagine that such glances had ever fallen,
abashed, before a fond or daring gaze, or been fused
into oneness with it, yet Anastasia would have understood to its nethermost such a gaze; she could have
translated it with Irish phrases and endearments
that had the pang of devotion in them—phrases
that flash as softly as a grey sea that the sun gazes

upon suddenly through slow clouds. What she would not have understood is the physical love, frosted cunningly with spiritual, that is the romance of to-day; if any downfall of virtue shook her community (and rarely was it so shaken), she said, in chorus with her fellows, " Why wouldn't she mind herself? "

When Anastasia tended the sick, as she did at intervals through the night, she was clumsy in movement yet swift, perceptive yet unmoved, patient, but from philosophy rather than from that tenderness that has its heart within the need of its tended one.

The night had clouded over, and when the dawn came it was a long and gentle growth of greyness, without a sunrise in it. The song of the robin trickled through the stillness, like a string of little silver beads across a sad embroidery; at the other side of the river a bell in the whitewashed convent intoned in a clear treble, and christened the day to its faith and purpose. The quiet hopelessness of the sick-room ceased to be the central thing in life; others were travelling on the same road and would reach the same gate.

Anastasia had gone out to the kitchen, where activities of an intermittent sort had sprung up. A girl was rattling tin cans, and humming a song that I had heard before :

> " Oh, I bought my love a dandy cap,
> Oh yes, indeed, a dandy cap;
> I bought my love a dandy cap,
> With eight and thirty borders.

> " *Oh, beela shula geelahoo,*
> *Oh, gra machree, for ever you,*
> *Oh, beela shula geelahoo,*
> *Indeed you are my darling.*

> " Oh, I wish I was in Galway Town,
> Oh yes, indeed, in Galway Town;
> I wish I was in Galway Town,
> It's there I'd meet my darling."

It was a minor air, that swayed in low and persistent dejection. There was a pause, while the tin cans clanked again in time to a jovial footstep, and I saw the songster at the edge of the river. She slapped her cans on to the water, and the stream plunged into them and pulled them under, and she pulled them forth from it easily, though she was slight, with small, fine hands. She sat down at the brink and began to scour a wooden bowl with river sand and a wisp of straw, lilting " Lanigan's Ball," and scouring in time to its elastic rhythm. A young man in a creamy flannel bauneen and a soft black hat came riding down the opposite bank on a bare-backed, yellow Connemara pony, and splashed out into midstream (and, incidentally, into the spawning-bed that there resided). The yellow pony stretched forth her neck and laid her black lip on the sliding current. " Lanigan's Ball " did not cease.

" Mary Ellen," said the young man, leaning back with his hand on the mare's quarter while she drew the water up her long throat, " I'm goin' to be married this Shraft, and I'll give you the preference."

Mary Ellen glanced up at him with ethereal grey eyes, from under wisps of auburn hair.

" Thank ye, Johnny, I'd sooner stay as I am," she replied, as if she were declining the loan of an umbrella, and instantly and blithely resumed the interrupted phrase of " Lanigan's Ball," with its whirling sand and straw obligato.

The yellow pony splashed and stumbled through the spawning-bed, and returned to the further shore.

" Maybe it's looking for me on Shrove Tuesday you'll be," said her rider, over his shoulder, as he ascended the opposite bank.

Mary Ellen lilted and scoured, and in due season returned to the house.

After her return, conversation arose in the kitchen, and immediately throve; there was long-drawn laughter, with Anastasia as humorist; it was comfortable to hear it.

In the grass between the window and the river the young spikes of the daffodils were grouped like companies of spearmen, resolute in the cold opposition of January. A thorn-tree leaned stiffly over the hastening water, and the robin that had been drinking near its roots shot up, as if tossed from the ground, accomplished a lofty curve, and sank again, in exquisite transitory yielding to the earth-force that would some day defeat it for ever. The low wind gathered purpose, and a mist began to thicken the sky. It went and came, as though it must return to press the house to its bosom, and tell those within of its love and its despondency.

MARTIN ROSS.

1914.

A DELEGATE OF THE NATIONAL LEAGUE

His new workshop is a disaster in the landscape, an incident unsurpassingly dreary even in a region whose buildings cannot be said to sweeten the rigours of bog-stretches and mountain-side; a structure to which no beholder will grudge the award of being the most unattractive in the parish, even after attention has been given to the claims of the chapel and the national schools. It is its fate to have many beholders, swinging and jolting by, most of them on the Connemara mail-cars, within a few yards of it, where it commands the entrance of a boreen, and noting it, no doubt, with all the curious gaze of the tourist. To these it will readily recall the goods-store of any railway-station on their journey in its solidity of stone and slate and gloomy adherence to the necessary; and those of a Charles Dickens turn of mind will discern the sore-eyed stare imparted to it by the setting of red bricks round its windows. But, fortunately for it, it has another class of beholders, less practised of eye and altogether innocent of such imaginings. To the people in the knot of cabins among the trees behind, it is a thing of utmost note and significance, an architectural idyll in which is voiced all that they can desire of fitness and perfection, which proclaims to the world at large, as it defiles past on its mail-cars, that some one of their cabin roofs shelters the intellect and prosperity capable of such an achievement.

It is not a long time since the village and the

neighbourhood in general spent many happy hours of idleness in looking on at the erection of the workshop—idleness of the fascinating kind that borrows occupation from the toil of another, and is conducive

THE DELEGATE

to the making of gratuitous comment and the consumption of tobacco. From previous knowledge of the intelligence that devised and carried out the building, it may be conjectured how such advice would be received; probably with the mere protrusion of a nether lip, or even, more possibly, with grimmest unconcern, while the Delegate's quick hands joined rafter to roof-tree. Thirty years of unquestioned supremacy in matters of carpentering, and perhaps in some other matters, might give a reasonable contempt for the opinions of those who in a like period have been supreme in nothing, unless it be in the ordering of their pig-sties.

To-day the workshop is closed, and walking past it up the lane, there is nothing to be heard of the cheerful din of hammer and scream of saw. Unfinished cart-wheels lie about the door, and the delegate's bay filly has hung her head over the wall of the field in con-templation of these, and of an outside car which stands in evil plight, tilted back on its springs, with a broken shaft pointing skywards. She is evidently satisfied that this stillest of October days is nothing less than the Sabbath, and that the heavy cart-straddle which has already hollowed her three-year-old back will not to-day be placed there. As to the day of the week she is mistaken, but some feeling of suspension there certainly is, of pause or interval in which village life has been arrested, with the exception of a solitary village cock, whose crows now and again supplicate the foggy stillness for an answer.

The Delegate's cottage cannot architecturally be compared with his workshop—in fact, it only escapes the designation of cabin by virtue of possessing three windows, and the almost unknown departure of a flower-garden, a three-cornered jungle, where goose-berry-bushes and double dahlias dispute every inch of ground behind a sufficiently neat paling. The door of the house is open as usual, and from the semi-darkness within comes a murmur of voices, hushed but incessant, with an interspersed groan or two which meets the ear on entering. The earthen floor is extremely uneven to any but an accustomed foot, and a smoky dimness above in the peak of the rafters shows that the delegate's advanced ideas found their whole expression in the workshop, and did not intrude on the sanctities of home in aspiring to a chimney better constructed than other people's. Opaqueness of atmosphere, however, is as ordinary a circumstance of life to the dozen or so of women now inhaling it as are the dampness and inequality of the floor on which they are squatting, in attitudes suggestive of races more remote from civilisation. The subject in hand is too engrossing to receive anything but the most trifling check at the new arrival, and the voluble western Irish gurgles on in undertones, with noddings of shawled heads, moving pendulum-like with the flow of harangue. A very small knowledge of Irish makes it easy to understand that they are, in the immemorial way, rehearsing the benevolences and talents of the newly dead; and the feeling of pause that hung about the silent workshop deepens here round the catastrophe of a few hours ago.

The woman who is of right the chief mourner of this gathering leads the way into the next room, and pointing to the heavy bed in the corner, says, without tears or even any apparent heroic suppression of them : "There he is for you. What do you think of him now ? "

Whatever is thought is not likely to be of much moment, but at all events the answer cannot be a ready one. At dawn he was still a delegate of the National League, not perhaps as much interested in it and its doctrines as it was his wont to be, not indeed interested in anything except whatever things they were of which he occasionally muttered to himself while life sank away from him in the growing daylight. His name may now be crossed out in the League

c

accounts; and patriot oratory may belabour the name of Balfour with highest-piled epithet, without altering by a hair's breadth the humorousness which in some way has lingered into rigidity about the lips of the dead man. The room is not darkened, but the small window tempers the light to a most fitting uncertainty, not tampering with the expression shadowed under pent-house brows, but softening it to its habitual strong attentiveness.

The hazy sunshine outside has struck on a red dahlia at the window, and the brilliant note of colour draws the eye to it out of the grave obscurity of the room. It was at this window that the delegate used to sit after his day's work, studying indefatigably the newspaper utterances of his party, American and otherwise, and forming thereon opinions of the crudeness which might be expected from an eager mind unfurrowed by any ploughshare of opposite opinion. But it is not difficult to imagine that such as he might occasionally raise his eyes from the columns of vituperation, and look out over his gooseberry-bushes and dahlias to where the cloud of rooks wheels in the sunset over adjacent demesne lands and woods, with feelings of a mixed and bewildered kind. Many incidents of his life rising up from the background of these woods would parry irrationally the cut and thrust of Socialism; perhaps even such trivial memories as the wooden swords and other playthings made in bygone days for certain children of the vituperated class would for a time confuse the political outlook, and leave the Delegate at length floundering a little in the problem of the old order *versus* the new. Such flounderings can only be guessed at; whether they were many or few, he did not, so far as can be known, trouble his neighbours with the recital of them; but by a solitary circumstance some glimpse into a mind divided against itself shall not be wanting.

The chapel in which the parish hears its Mass said once a week is a building set on a hill, presenting its whitewashed sides and blank windows as a spectacle for much surrounding country. Brown mountains look to it across a ribbon of lake, a wide expanse of bog spreads sombre-hued to the bases of the nearer slopes, and eastward, between lake and lake, is a weird stretch of country where the rocks stand thicker in every field till greenness is crushed out, and desolation stark and stony meets the horizon. Straggling from and through such improbable surroundings comes on each Sunday a congregation that is quite enough for the capabilities of the chapel, converging from all points of the compass in Sunday frieze or red petticoats, in numbers which might seem imposing to a man whose world they represent. Picture, then, on a Sunday of some years ago, the Delegate among this company, folded in with the rest of the flock by four whitewashed walls, and occupying a position by no means obscure; having, in fact, laid his hat by the altar-rails, and stationed himself not further from it than is usual. Mass having been said, some matters not strictly ecclesiastical are touched on in the address that follows, and these finally come under discussion of a general sort. They at length, and with much admixture of personal allusion and detail, merge themselves into question relating to the demesne lands mentioned elsewhere, and the propriety of allowing a certain grazier to rent them for his cattle. There is apparently but one mind among the disciples of liberty, and one word expresses it—boycott; but that things may be done with due decorum, the spiritual adviser puts the matter to the vote. The equivalent for assent in the Irish language marks without a variation the progress of the question down the line of faces till only three or four remain, and here, where least expected, a volcanic upheaval shatters the smooth unanimity.

Fourth from the end sits the Delegate, with an expression which, to onlookers less confident of their man, might have been portentous, biding his time in silence, while the accumulating verdict travels to him. His answer is not contained in one word nor in a few; it is declaimed with excitement amounting to fierceness, and is to the effect that at least his vote shall not sanction the contemplated tyranny. Persuasive remonstrance is trampled on and swallowed up by a demand as to whether it is at the mandate of the National League that the grass grows up through the ground for the use of cattle, and whether it lies with that body to deprive it of its mission. Receiving no answer, he does not insist on one, but, snatching his hat from the altar-rails, he walks down through the crowded chapel, and out of it with, perhaps, as great an air as any of Ireland's representatives have attained to when quitting the House of Commons in obedience to its decree, and followed, as may be conjectured, by a congregational gaze of extreme blankness.

It might be supposed that such an episode would have been followed by results of a marked kind— results the reverse of pleasing to the Delegate and his possessions, with perhaps, on his part, a reactionary hurling of himself into the camp of the opposite party; or that, at best, his defection from his own would have been passed over as a forgivable eccentricity, a discordancy which would be easily drowned in the patriot pronouncements. But supposition is marvellously set at naught. The Delegate sits by his window and reads his newspaper as of old, without let or hindrance, or any black looks cast aslant at him by the passers-by; and the evening shadows of the trees flicker in their accustomed way over sanguinary paragraphs and daring editorial utterances. Stranger still, the shadows of some other trees fall day after day on the grazier's cattle taking their noonday shelter, or roving through them from bracken to pasture; and the excommunicated grass is cropped in peace, and the Damocles sword, which presumably menaces each grazing head, hangs impalpable in the ether, neither descending with mutilations of the customary sort, nor in any way hindering the creditable sleekness of the herd at the October fair.

The hidden connections of these things are not easily arrived at—perhaps, indeed, of all concerned, the cattle alone knew clearly their own minds and motives, but, looking now at the Delegate, the mystery of unconscious personal influence seems to unfold itself, the secret of the strength which, whether uncertain of motive or not, could draw to itself without an effort many blinder intelligences. It is not hard to believe that his convictions would be a vigorous offspring, courageous in their grasp of things, in the light of whose guidance his neighbours and friends would walk with an accustomed faith; and the realisation follows of the stout-heartedness which could, in the most public way possible for it, dishonour its own intellect, and leave its convictions unfathered and disbanded in the sight of all men.

His spiritual adviser has fastened round his throat something resembling a black choker—a religious symbol of some kind, no doubt; a confession of helplessness quite out of keeping with the face above, which gives no hint that death had been too great a thing for it. Thus for two days he lies there, still in the position of host and central attraction of the crowd that nightly fills his house, perhaps lying there forgotten in the hilariousness that comes in the small hours of a wake, with the candles waning at his head and feet, and his lips apparently repressing much humour of an inscrutable sort.

His funeral is thought by those attending it to be the greatest sight ever seen in the district. Till a late hour in the afternoon the bohireen is trodden into mud by the hobnailed boots, horse-hoofs, and bare feet of the gathering assemblage, and down by the workshop some rickety outside cars wait to take their places in the procession. Outside the house of mourning, under the trees and the gloomy sky, stands a table, white-draped and cheerless, with the Delegate's best dinner-plate laid upon it. On the plate is a low heap of half-crowns and smaller silver, placed there by the guests, each of whom, male and female, receives in recognition a glass of whisky. It is not, however, in payment for the whisky that awkward fingers toss down their shillings and half-crowns; a matter of infinite moment is contained in the act, even such a thing as the repose of the Delegate's soul. Could he but look with bodily eyes from his coffined darkness, how would he regard the little silver heap, the amount that his friends will spare to shape for him a bulwark against the unknown terror? Possibly with more stoicism than others might, and with the added reflection that for no one else in the country would the heap have been so large.

The Irish cry is becoming a little old-fashioned even in Connemara, and there are only a few women competent to uplift it when the coffin is at length carried down the bohireen; but these do not spare themselves in the raising of the dirge, and sway theatrically to its rhythm in their walk. The coffin is thus carried for a short distance only on its four-mile journey, being at the foot of the first hill transferred to a cart of cheerful agricultural hues, drawn by a shaggy chestnut, against whose unresenting flank its projecting bulk is pressed. The chief mourners scramble in after it, and without any thought of incongruity or unfitness, seat themselves on the coffin itself, back to back, in a deplorable-looking row. About the cart as it moves away, and behind it for a quarter of a mile, straggles confusedly the funeral crowd, to the number of two or three hundred, many of them stumbling from a too-evident cause, but preserving, to do them justice, a demeanour of seemly gloom; and as they pass along the road, a villainous whisky reek spreads itself on the pure bog air.

The cart comes to a standstill at the entrance gates of an avenue, in which the Delegate's figure was once as familiar an object as the owner's; and here, as at a fitting opportunity, the keeners lift their cry for a moment or two. The chestnut moves on again, and the crowd straggles broadcast behind it; while above their heads rises as a last impression the figure of the Delegate's daughter, with red hair streaming dishevelled, and arms flung to the grey sky. Some vision of her father, striding actively to those entrance-gates, as in the old times, with his easily-balanced head and commanding height, must have driven her to her feet, and transfixed her thus, Niobe-like, above the sodden throng that follows with decorously suppressed hiccoughings and an occasional solemn stagger. Her arms seem as if lifted in bearing testimony of some kind, and it is, perhaps, a prejudiced fancy that further endows the gesture with an acknowledgment of the affection that bound gentleman and peasant in the days held in small estimation by the National League.

One other acknowledgment finds its place at the

" THERE HE IS FOR YOU. WHAT DO YOU THINK OF HIM NOW ? "

last. When the people stand round the grave at sunset, and see the coffin lowered out of sight of lake and hills, the white flowers of a cross look back to them from below. It is not a tribute from the National League, nor do such flowers grow in cabin-gardens; and they now take the mould on their freshness as quietly as if satisfied that they have proclaimed the endurance of an old friendship.

MARTIN ROSS.

July 1889.

CHEOPS IN CONNEMARA

EDUCATION is a fine word, a word charged with respectable associations. Whether pronounced as here written, or in its other varieties of ejjication or eddication, its weightiness is felt to be very great, even if it is variously comprehended; indeed, it has in this respect a position somewhat more assured than religion. Coupled with the word national, it has been much and skilfully bandied about the pages of reviews, with a sound as of heaviest artillery, wonderfully in contrast to the docile lispings or tearful whinings of the daily task, whose present or future purport is what all this noise is about.

From the thunder of such conflicts the ordinary ignoramus respectfully conceals himself, believing, in common with a great many of his class, that such things are generally settled for the best somehow after the noise is over, and not trying overmuch to realise where cause ends and effect begins in the minds of school children. Certainly such questions are far from the mind of one of this sort, who, on a gloomy afternoon, takes his way into a solitude where it would seem that education might wander as a forlorn thing and find no resting-place. Wisdom herself might cry to the surrounding desolation from the outside car which is creeping along through it in the teeth of a bullying blast from the Atlantic, and catch no reply, or even echo of her summons.

Moor or bog, it is hard to know which to call it; a brown and billowy waste without any hint of

boundary, its farthest ridges fading into haze, its
nearer hollows seamed with a black or green swampi-
ness; and far and near, sunk in the heather or cresting
the slopes, lie weather-whitened boulders, scattered
supine, like a fossil herd of cattle. In the complete
absence of any other thing to look at, a good deal
of time is spent in speculating as to what kind of
eruptive effort or watery subsidence strewed the
country over with these improbable rocks; and as
the car jolts along the levels and crawls over the short
ridges, the problem becomes so oppressive that a
wish is almost formed for the presence of the abhorred
schoolboy and his geology primer. The carman
gives it as his opinion that " thim was in it since the
race of man "; but this is clearly impromptu, a creditable attempt to meet a question never before imagined.
His next piece of information is that just half of this
desert has been crossed; but by what subtlest
recognition he is aware of it, it is hard to imagine.
Around lie the dead monotonies, the misty, deceptive
horizon, so bare of incident and so bereft of life that
the thin road flung across its undulations has something of the vigour and solitary daring of a line of rails
in Central Asian steppes; or even, with long looking
at, comes to mean a living creature traversing an
enchanted land.

But as the horse surmounts the slope from which
this survey has been made, there appears, in the
hollow beyond, an object as unexpected as one of
these boulders of rock would be in Bond Street. It
is a small house, immaculately whitewashed and
slated, standing out from the side of the hill with the
wind singing everlastingly about its roof, and snatching
away its thread of turf smoke before it can humanise
the landscape. Above its brilliant green door a
board with the legend " —— National School " tells

that here, in undreamed-of waters, education has let down her net for a draught. What is therein enclosed we shall see.

At a distance of some thirty yards the sound of many voices makes itself heard—a chorus of childish brogues, declaiming something or other with a fervour and unanimity worthy of a Crystal Palace oratorio; and when a pause is made to listen, it seems as if words of a sacred sort recur in the clamour. The children are standing inside in small rings, bellowing into each other's faces with the utmost heartiness; but the sudden tendency of many eyes to the open door is followed by such a perceptible diminuendo that there appears in the doorway the teacher herself, to see what is the matter—a young person with a cast-iron black fringe, a useful-looking wand of office, and an eye fraught with the multiplication-table. Amplest apologies for the disturbance are graciously accepted, even to the extending of an invitation to come in and see the school; and accepting this the stranger steps straightway into a long room filled from end to end with children. Hair of every shade is the general impression on looking down the room; heads sleek or shaggy, flaxen or black, with a flaming red here and there; and from beneath each a steadfast upward gaze is fastened on the visitor. The spell of Central Asian solitude is broken up, the fairy-tale road is the familiar highway for a hundred pairs of bare feet; all is reduced to simplicity, except the question of where the children come from.

The teacher, having explained that religious instruction is just over, offers the visitor a window-sill—there being no chair in the school—and proceeds to marshal her choicest pupils for examination. A book is produced entitled *Sixth Reading-book for the Use of Schools*, and turning it over, the eye is caught by extracts from *Paradise Lost,* from Pope's *Essay on Criticism,* from Paley's *Relation of Animated Bodies to Inanimate Nature,* from apparently most of the recognised classics. Looking up from this at a sound of bare feet on the boards, the visitor sees stationed before the judicial window-seat a tattered and unkempt boy, who smiles and hangs down his head with the most ingenuous shyness.

" Martin Griffy, repeat the ' Address to a Mummy,' " says the teacher in her carefully-repressed brogue; and fixing his eyes upon his own muddy toes, Martin Griffy forthwith embarks upon that poem, in a voice pitched to the level of intoning and there conscientiously sustained.

Most people are familiar with Horace Smith's kindly attempt to provide a mummy in Belzoni's Exhibition with a history of its own; few, perhaps, are favoured to hear it thus rendered, carefully, correctly, but as in an unknown tongue, the guesses of modern erudition coming in staccato sing-song from the lips of a child who, it is most probable, has never seen a town, knows of no fuel but that of his native bogs, and only suspects that there is a completer kind of daily food than potatoes and tea. Much less does he suspect the subtle and penetrating pathos of his looks and his endeavour. Those who have felt the anxiety and effort of a dog who walks round a circus on his hind-legs, will know that it is touching to see a mind obediently bent to the doing of what is foreign to it. The poem progresses: Cheops and Cephrenes, Cambyses and Osiris are got over with occasional quaintness of pronunciation, and the auditor contrives to take a look at the glossary at the end of the book to see what is said about these names of antiquity. He finds there a great deal of scholarly comment, as, for instance, " *Thebes,* an

Egyptian city, not to be confounded with the Thebes in Greece;" "Osiris, Orus, Apis, Isis, divinities worshipped by the heathen Egyptians," but notices also a little capriciousness in selection, Cheops, Cambyses, and many others being passed over without any explanation.

The recitation is brought to a most creditable ending. Martin Griffy answers, in the language of the glossary, some questions upon it, and other pupils are brought forward—a fiery-haired girl with unpleasant green eyes, and a boy of ten, dressed in a long white flannel petticoat, according to the humiliating custom of the country with small boys. Searching problems in arithmetic and geography are disposed of by these with admirable speed, and finally the dreaded moment comes—the stranger is invited to put a few questions to the pupils. In desperation he asks the date of the Norman invasion. Dead silence and a communing of glances is the result, and the teacher looks extremely blank. On explaining the question to her, she says that no history is taught in the school; no history is taught in any Irish National School so far as she is aware. She seems to think the subject insignificant, and on reflection it appears better not to inquire further into it at this time. But a little later, when turning to go, a mixture of feeling about it makes the final glance down the long room a somewhat melancholy one.

The horse is roused from a laborious luncheon of dwarfish roadside grass; the teacher stands in the doorway and says farewell with a graciousness expanded to enthusiasm by the latest encomium in the visitors' book, all unaware of the sentiment with which the writer of it is regarding her as the car moves away; complacently unconscious of the incongruity of her own face and elaborate fringe, framed in the whitewashed aperture, with immensities of horizon and wind and solitude overwhelming her.

It is not many miles now to the Atlantic; its saltness is already in the wind, and the chains of the traces clank loosely as the horse leans back against his harness on the long downward stretch of road that will find its ending in a little street, a strip of civilisation existing and growing between the wilderness and the sea, with a kind of vegetable persistence and stillness. The last half-hour of jolting does not seem long, and the mind is no longer affaired with speculations as to the empty silences and void places of the earth. It is filled instead with the clatter of school hours, with the solitary voice reciting carefully the possibilities of the mummy's previous life, and with a great wonder as to the shape in which such things stow themselves away in the brain of such childhood as is here. It is not easy to picture the guise in which Cheops, Osiris and the rest pass before the minds that can give them no other stage than the native bog and moor—the necessary background for all imaginations of theirs—no better stage-properties than the furniture of a two-roomed cabin, and the flannel and frieze of Connemara. Like solitary enigmas, these and kindred things must show themselves, uncomprehended and unquestioned as is the evening glimmer of stars by the eyes that, looking dully upwards from cabin doors, see the points of light kindling where all before was impenetrable blue.

A sea fog has begun to cling about the expanses of heather and bog, and the white rocks show through the greyness like touches of foam on a wide and gloomy sea. The desolation behind is wrapped in a more mysterious desolateness; the sense of remoteness is quickened, till something is felt of the true value of distance, of the old-fashioned significance of it to those whose world still lies within their longest walk. But the limitations of that world are more than ever felt when the desired goal is reached at length, the metropolis of the surrounding waste, with its sufficiently decent cottages, and more than sufficient supply of public-houses. On the stony sands below it lie, keel upwards (if they can be said to have a keel), the coracles—slight frames of wood, with tarred canvas stretched over them, in which most of the fishing is done. It is as if to make their safety seem more marvellously improbable that, in the wildness of this twilight, the Atlantic rollers come towering to the beach, and fall there with as separate a circumstance and ruin as the walls of Jericho.

MARTIN ROSS.

October 1889.

QUARTIER LATINITIES (I)

TEN milk-cans, five on each side of the doorway, repel the sunshine of the Boulevard Mont Parnasse from their clouded and battered sides. Half-a-dozen apples are in one window, some sallow *serviettes* in rings in the other, along with a bowl of eggs dyed red as radishes, and moving selectively among them, there is usually the hand and arm of the proprietor. Those whose appetite can be discomfited by the sight of a dirty hand will certainly seek their dinner elsewhere; but these eccentrics are not prevalent in the Quartier Latin, and certainly occupy no place in the calculations of the proprietor.

Monsieur of the *crêmerie* does not, indeed, trouble himself at all with the trivialities of personal appearance, nor, if an outsider may venture to express an opinion, do his customers seem to be greatly concerned on the subject. Behind his counter of a yard long stands Monsieur, watchful as his own big grey cat, and marks, with Heaven knows what allotment to to-morrow's soup, those portions of the *côtelettes* that the company have found uneatable, even while he supplies outdoor customers with half-pennyworths of milk, ladled out with a lavish lift of the hand that suggests anything rather than the retention of the last teaspoonful in the bottom of the measure. He also, from the tail of his black eye, can survey the rites of his female subordinates in the kitchen, a privilege that will not be grudged to him by those who have chanced to perceive Angélique preparing a plate for prunes and cream by sousing it and its grisly remnants of beefsteak in a vat behind the kitchen door. If one wishes to dine with a quiet mind for anything under two francs it is better not to have glimpses of the machinery; better to sit down in a corner where none such are possible, and to fix one's attention on the little wooden spade that holds the *ménu*. Its handle feels greasy; so, for the

MONSIEUR OF THE *CRÊMERIE*

matter of that, does the handle of the knife, but it is only the new-comer who finds such things remarkable.

Round the other tables there is a spasmodic prattle of English and American female voices, spasmodic because subordinate to the earnest consumption of the *crêmerie's* inevitable beefsteak and mutton chops; but the studio " still lisps out in all they utter," the place to buy canvases, the iniquities of the model, legends of those artists whose dismal duty it is to pass judgment weekly on the works of the speakers; these, and much more, interspersed with calls for

Angélique, as unceasing as the entreaties of the worshippers of Baal for a manifestation. Apparently, like Baal, Angélique sleeps, or is on a journey; or is it that she is the object of a halting badinage from the American young gentlemen in the inner room? There is a glass partition, and looking through it, the eye is suddenly confronted by a hairy yellow jaw, and a shirt collar which doubtless made a brave show on its *début* last Sunday week. Its owner is eating cream cheese, with fresh cream and sugar over it, in gloomy abstraction. He certainly is not the humorist of the moment. Beyond his Jewish nose and eyeglasses are several profiles, all bent upon Angélique, who, infinitely affaired with plates of fried potatoes and cauliflower, is yielding a slight mechanical coquetry as the due of the jest in its raucous American-French. The humorist is a young gentleman who has formed himself as nearly as possible on the model of the French art student, by the simple device of allowing his hair to grow, brushing up his moustache, and abjuring soap. He is conscious of success in the character, and Angélique concedes him a smile which surely singles him out as one of the elect. A little more, and he will tuck a napkin into his collar at meals, and wear a short frock-coat with his blue velvet tam-o'-shanter.

With the exception of the misanthrope with the cream cheese, all, male and female, eat their six o'clock dinner with singular cheerfulness. Drawing gives an appetite, as those can vouch who have seen the eyes of the class waver gauntly towards the clock in the half-hour before *déjeuner*, and most of those at the *crêmerie* have drawn for eight hours to-day. Of this no one is more intelligently aware than Monsieur, and therefore does he confidently present, day after day, the same mutton chop with the long shank, and the fat made of indiarubber, the two square inches of beefsteak without any fat, concluding with cream cheese and prunes, a rigorous seven of the latter going to the portion. All is eaten; the little thick plate that makes the allowance of beefsteak and fried potatoes seem an overflowing mess of Benjamin is cleared to the last chip, to the last trawl of the fork in the gravy for the scrap of fried onion that never was there; sometimes the gravy itself is mopped up with bread, a thing not agreeable to see. The natives know better than their comrades how to extract the utmost from the bill of fare; they know that the *Chateaubriand* at sevenpence-halfpenny is not as good value as the ordinary beefsteak at fivepence, and they take the difference in a plate of spinach, or a salad, or a glass of black coffee that tastes of liquorice and sarsaparilla, but gives a feeling of having dined. The English, with true British belief in the expensive, take the *Chateaubriand*, and afterwards buy a half-pennyworth of . milk and pennyworth of bread, and go hungrily home to make tea.

It can be seen that prices at the *crêmerie* are moderate. It is possible to dine sufficiently for a single franc; satiatingly, with three courses and a bottle of *ordinaire,* for eighteenpence; it is also possible, on days when there is *bouilli* at threepence, to stay one's appetite for that sum. But in any case the forks and spoons will be more than dubious, the *serviettes* like pieces of coarse sheeting, and the eyes must be averted at the unescapable moment when the prune juice or the soup washes over Angélique's thumb as she puts down the plate with a swing. A memory rises of soup *à l'oseille*, that seductively-named potion, that looked like water in which the breakfast things had been washed,

UN BON GYMNASIARQUE (*p. 38*)

leaving tea-leaves and crusts of bread floating about in it. What it tasted like is a thing that its victim will struggle long and anxiously to forget. But how to remove the recollection of a slab of something that was entitled *tête de veau à la sauce Ravigote*, and resembled the unshaven cheek of an elderly gentleman? It is a matter too recent and poignant to dwell upon.

At the other side of the street is a *café* with little tables under its awning, and the white pinafores of the *garçons* flutter in the fresh spring wind as they flit about, supplying customers with rich, dark *ragoûts* and blue-green glasses of absinthe. It is named, in brilliant red letters, *Restaurant au Paradis des cochers*, and at an opposite corner stands another of its kind, dedicated in gold to the *Rendez-vous des bons Gymnasiarques*. The trees of the Boulevard already cast a grotto-like shade upon the little tables, and the fat men who sit at them. The *crêmerie* has no awning, no shading trees; its customers sit crowded on comfortless stools in a hot room. Why do we not hold *rendez-vous* with the good Gymnasiarques, those occult beings not to be found in Bellows' dictionary, or enter into the Paradise of the coachmen, and eat hen *au chasseur* and craggy lumps of roast lamb with *sauce au diable*?

No one attempts to answer the question, and at mid-day and at evening the same figures squeeze through the same narrow doorway, and the same voices beseech Angélique for the amaranthine *côtelette aux pommes frites*.

MARTIN ROSS.

November 1894.

QUARTIER LATINITIES (II)

EARLY or late, there is no silence in the Boulevard Mont Parnasse. Not even on Sunday morning after sunrise, when the dew hangs grey on the coloured wire wreaths in the cemetery close by, and the Eiffel Tower, asleep in the haze, might be Jacob's ladder awaiting the angels, or the sea-serpent standing on end. The rhythm of the tram-horses' hoofs has been scarcely forgotten in dreams before it has begun again, with its accompaniment of bleats upon the driver's horn; the *voitures* have not ceased to spin over the paving-stones when the monster carts enter on their day's work, rumbling like thunder, causing the very bed of the sleeper to tremble; the last shop has not slammed its doors before the first *crêmerie* has banged open its shutters; and through it all the conversation of passers-by has been a steady thread of connection.

Now, at eight o'clock, when nothing except the milkman has stirred the Sunday morning trance of Bayswater, the Boulevard Mont Parnasse is in the full swing of business. A man in blue linen, with panes of glass strapped on his back, is chanting the word, " *Vi-tri-er!* " in a strong nasal tenor, a boy is advertising goats' milk by a shrill tune played on a reed pipe, while his five black goat-ladies pace before him, discreet and cunning-eyed; two women are cleaning and re-making a wool mattress upon a large frame stretched under the trees; they stab it through

39

DURING THE WORKING-HOURS

and through with their immense needles as suddenly and viciously as if they were transfixing an enemy. The Boulevard is full of wheels, from the female cyclist flitting by in her hideous knickerbockers, to the cart drawn by five leviathan horses, with a tree thirty feet high, in full leaf, standing erect upon it; and in the thick of these, threading them with the stride and the boot-heel of an alien civilisation, is the art student. A tin milk-can swings from her bare hand, a long pennyworth of bread, slightly draped in tissue paper, is under her arm; the other hand grasps an orange, and the gloves that some superstitious recollection of the proprieties prompts her to carry. She has bought her breakfast an hour later than usual—Sunday being observed in her studio as a holiday—she will cook it over a spirit-lamp on her washhandstand, she will partake of it out of a tin cup, she will wash up the breakfast service with more or less conscientiousness, according to disposition, or the influence of religion, and then she will make her toilet.

Improbable as it may seem to those who see her only during the working hours of the week, she has distinct aspirations on the subject of dress. In obedience to an almost irresistible instinct of her kind she wears cinnamon-brown or myrtle-green gowns, cut very low at the neck, without any attempt to fill up deficiencies with lace or other washable materials; but the rock on which she splits is a fatal wavering between the artistic and the fashionable. Sir E. Burne-Jones and M. Puvis de Chavannes are possibly responsible for the cinnamon-brown or the myrtle-green hue of her garments, and also for the extent of neck which is left uncovered; but the Bon Marché's culpability is equal to theirs in placing on her straying locks the horse-shoes of acute magenta roses, the eccentric straw hats tufted with bunches of livid pink cowslips in which she may be seen taking her Sabbath airing.

Having, like the locust, no king, she goes forth by companies, and settles down upon the Parisian Sunday in swarms that devastate the *crêmeries* and suck the last *sou* of satisfaction out of concert or picture-gallery. Her male fellows merge more or less in the general ruck of life, and pass unconspicuous enough among the crowds of dirty youths who form the under-growth of the streets of the *Rive Gauche ;* but the Anglo-Saxon female, whether English or American, never assimilates with the Frenchwoman, and is as unmistakable as she is ubiquitous.

It is a bright April Sunday, and at the door of the Châtelet Theatre is a *queue* of people, pushing as only fat Frenchwomen can push, planting their pointed heels upon the instep of the obnoxious with smiling precision; and in the midst of them is the art student, fighting her way in and up the interminable stairs with scarcely inferior skill. It is a great occasion— a Grieg concert, presided over by the Master himself— and having paid four francs for her seat, she means to have it. Her strength is as the strength of ten, she is hampered by no regard for her personal dignity, and the Châtelet stairs feel themselves scorned and worsted as she speeds up them. She can even bring some sense of failure home to the nimble harpies, who, with dyed locks tied up with pink ribbons, and hearts seared with the habit of plunder, dominate the corridors of French theatres. She declines their proffered footstools, she sits upon her coat, and her hat, too, if necessary (we have even known a member of the community who reserved for the theatre a specially high-crowned hat with which to increase the height of her seat). They understand her French even less than she understands theirs, but she makes

it admirably clear to them that they have met their
match, and that the *petit benefice* will never be yielded
by her.

Within the great theatre, squadrons of faces, and
lines of light, curve in tiers from dress-circle to top
gallery; even in the top gallery but one, the height,
and the slant of heads below, would make many
people giddy. It is very hot, so hot that for the first
five minutes the brain seems to boil, and a disposition
to burst into maniac laughter at the mere idea of
having paid to endure such misery is with difficulty
restrained; to reflect that eels become used to skinning
brings no solace; in such an atmosphere as this to be
skinned would seem the sole means of making life
endurable. Fans are going in all quarters of the house;
with the air at this temperature they must merely
produce a sense of friction. The art students leaven
the lump downwards as far as the amphitheatre, and
she to whom fortune has allotted us companion seats
seems to think little of either the heat or the height.
She has often sat in the topmost gallery, and even
now certain of her friends, seated in that dizzy circle
of Tophet, are signalling to her the envy of which she
is already pleasurably aware. They fan themselves
with their hats and eat a great many oranges; nevertheless they also seem to enjoy themselves.

All that is to be seen of Herr Grieg is a mop of
greyish hair round a small bald spot, but his music
can be heard to perfection, and it makes one forget
the heat. The art student enjoys herself tremendously.
She is an enthusiast about Grieg; she belabours the
floor with a broad boot sole and an energy that envelops
her and her neighbours in a cloud of dust and induces
a visible animosity in a young American gentleman
who sits in front. He has been at some pains to explain
to a servile female relative that he finds the per-

formance mediocre; he is aware of the value of his opinion, and has bestowed it on those around in a penetrating voice, so that contrary demonstration becomes an impertinence. At the close of the concert, when applause and calls for Grieg have become almost hysterical, he yields sufficiently to the infection to admit that it has been pretty good. Returning home on the tram the art student thinks out many things that she might have said loudly and ambiguously to her friends, things that would have made the American young man regret that he had ever been born into an unappreciative world.

But already Grieg and the Châtelet are fading into the background of a mind loaded with the problem of whether to buy a tin of sardines and a bunch of radishes for dinner, or a couple of hard-boiled eggs and a penny tart. The Sunday dinner at the restaurant is not for those who have spent four francs on a concert; on the altar of the spirit-lamp she must offer an expiatory cup of cocoa to the offended economies, solitary except for the companionship of many promenading footsteps under the trees below, or the electric star of the Eiffel, flashing red and green in the dusky sky opposite her window. Even already a piano upstairs has begun to *réchauffer* the concert, and for many weeks the din of the Boulevard Mont Parnasse is surmounted by the noise of battle with Grieg's Holberg Suite.

MARTIN ROSS.

December 1894.

QUARTIER LATINITIES (III)

JOSTLE your way as rapidly as may be out of the
Rue Vavin, cross the Rue d'Assas, and pass through
the little corner gate into the Luxembourg Gardens.
What a breath of young grass and hawthorn in blossom
to replace the oniony whiff of the third-rate restaurant,
the pent staleness of the narrow street! This is the
freshest and most pastoral corner of the gardens,
where large trees lean down to touch the grass,
unvexed by lopping or strict relation to their neighbours, where a hamlet of beehives has a grove to
itself, and there are no flower-beds. But it is not
popular; only the sourest of the *bonnes*, the most
select of the children, the moodiest of the idlers,
take their pleasure here among the horse-chestnuts
and copper beeches; even the dogs know it to be a
mere health resort, and mope obediently along upon
their leashes with a demeanour shorn of gallantry.
It is at the other side of the gardens, where prim alleys
of young trees spring geometrically from acres of
gravel, and the merry-go-round circles everlastingly
to a muffled internal tune, that the world of fashion
is to be found. There are many seats among the thin
tree-stems, and each groans beneath its load of nurses,
babies, and underlings of the nurse; family parties
sit in circles on hired chairs, conversing with amazing
zest round perambulators, both double and single;
little girls ply their skipping-ropes like clockwork.
Here it is that French domestic life, long maligned,
shows itself in colours as gratifying as unexpected,

transcending our vaunted English variety. It is not only that the father of the family tolerates his offspring in a public and cheerful manner, a condescension which we esteem almost touching; here, unwearied, he whirls the skipping-rope for the skipping of his yellow-faced daughters, he conciliates the baby in its most apoplectic paroxysm of spleen, he holds long and beautifully histrionic conversations with his mother-in-law and his great-aunt by marriage. He is a pattern even to Mr. Fairchild, who, to the best of my recollection, was in the habit of "stretching himself on the grass, at a little distance, with his book," when his children had tea and anecdotes out-of-doors. Even from this paragon among parents Mrs. Sherwood expected no more.

It is interesting to discover what a dislike can in the course of an hour be cultivated for the nurse, the omnipotent *Nou-nou*, with her immense coloured ribbons streaming from the back of her white cap, her black eyes that observe all things, her obesity, her offensive and unembarrassed familiarity with her mistress, her innumerable allies, and the detonating kisses with which she greets them. She pervades the Luxembourg Gardens from their opening to their closing, in violation of every English tradition of nursery hours and seasons. From beneath the hawthorns on the terrace she investigates the passer-by with a practised eye; along the straight alleys she advances with a slow and swaying stride. The female children skip to the exclusion of all other amusements; every vista is alive with their heads bobbing up and down; their thin legs leap from the gravel as if from a spring-board; their pale cheeks do not flush. Those who are too young to skip sit in the dust and collect it into heaps in the primeval manner. It was, indeed, my privilege to see an excessively naughty little girl fill a paper bag with surreptitious handfuls of it and empty it into the perambulator of a friend's baby, while the *Nou-nous* were lost in a blind ecstasy of conversation. No one but the baby witnessed the outrage, and the baby's eye was that of a cónspirator. Whether the culprit was eventually brought to justice I cannot say. My opinion of her intelligence inclines me to the belief that she was not.

Taken as a class, the girls are the superiors of the boys in the art of playing. They skip to perfection; they are full of detail and mystery in their dust grubbings; they are nimble, fearless and subtle. But what could be more lamentable than the endeavour of a French boy to throw a ball, unless it be his endeavour to catch it ? What more futile than his manner of jumping, his prancing run ? what more hopeless than his own complete satisfaction with these performances ? He is not decorative, with his thick, bare calves and his enveloping black pinafore; but he has a goblin intelligence, a pretty manner with his elders, and he rides with extravagant daring the horses that rock backwards and forwards on springs next door to the merry-go-round.

Under the trees near the terrace stands the booth of a Punch and Judy, with a small roped enclosure in front of it. Early in the afternoon the proprietress arranges chairs and benches for the spectators, and then sits down in front of the curtain to wait for an audience. She has a full, threatening eye, a slight grey moustache, and the stride of a Field-Marshal. It is not surprising that her husband, stationed at the other side with a harp, should be a weak-kneed, amiable person, who would let children sneak in under the rope if he dared. Most assuredly he does not dare; his part is to preface the entertainment with a meek mazurka on his harp, and to close it by rattling a box of coppers along the line of spectators outside the rope. Judging by the expression of his wife's eye, she has but little opinion of his conduct in these small matters. Both within and without the rope the audience is always large and unfailingly appreciative;

HIS PART IS TO PREFACE THE ENTERTAINMENT WITH
A MEEK MAZURKA ON HIS HARP

the dark eyes of the children on the benches glitter with intelligence, and their thin laughter responds shrilly and instantly to the Parisian volubilities of " *M. Guignol*," and the eldritch screeches of his baby. The outside audience does not disdain an equal sympathy, composed though it is of young men in tall hats, elderly ladies, and *cuirassiers* in the pomp of brass helmets with flowing horsehair plumes; they peer over each other's shoulders, they shout with delight at the crowning moment when the baby's mattress is sent skimming forth over their heads by "*M. Guignol's*" devastating flipper. Their backs, crowded close, are dark as a hiving swarm round the enclosure, and in spite of the defiance of the proprietress' eye, she well knows what an air of fashion is imparted by the non-paying spectators, what a magnetic influence upon families promenading afar among the aisles of bare tree-stems.

The French public, as it is seen in these gardens, cannot indeed be described as *blasé* or effete in the matter of amusing itself. This may be gay, wicked Paris; but here, beneath a horse-chestnut tree all alight with tiers of red blossom, three fashionable beings in frock-coats and floating neckties are playing battledore and shuttlecock and rolling a hoop. At a little distance a fourth, with shouts of laughter, dandles an air-balloon, and puffs out his fat, bearded cheeks to blow it upwards; while his white Pomeranian, clipped to the ridiculous semblance of a lion, regards him from a chair with the expression of an elderly and wearied governess. Beside the statue of a Grecian lady, who has the air of having taken the wrong medicine, a widow in stiff crape lappets is throwing a big painted ball on the ground and catching it in her arms as it bounds; she has done it so often that she has become unpleasantly warm.

Well, it has not always been child's play in the Luxembourg Gardens. These hawthorns that make a coolness along the balustrade of the terrace doubtless were in a similar reverie of fragrance and bloom on the bright Sunday in May when the Communists were taken out here from their court-martial in the Palace and shot *en masse* while the long daylight lasted, men and women, black with powder and the soot of conflagration. The man playing with the air-balloon

E

probably remembers it well; many of the ears now strained to catch the witticisms of *Guignol* must have heard the fusillade, and worse things than it. It is incredible. The faces of the children, sailing boats in the pond below, are not more concentrated on the present than those of their elders, not more unconscious of a past; the Luxembourg hawthorns and chestnuts have infinitely more suggestion about them of recollecting, of understanding.

MARTIN ROSS.

January 1895.

QUARTIER LATINITIES (IV)

IF there are those who desire to study a phase of currency that has escaped the notice of the bi-metallists, let them turn aside into the Quartier Latin, and behold the apotheosis of the *sou*. In the grey and graceless streets that pour their contribution of dirty people into the Rue de Rennes, or exhale their heavy breath round the Mont Parnasse cemetery, the *Napoleon* seems to belong to a forgotten mythology, the *franc* has a sinecure as the mere parent of coppers, and shop-fronts, *cabarets*, and *crêmeries* are decked in honour of the *centime*, are thronged by those whose lives are daily renewed through the utterance of the halfpenny.

A short expedition in the Rue de la Gaieté can be very enlightening on these points, especially if the hour be one of those hurrying ones between eight o'clock and *déjeuner*. To walk on the pavement is all but impossible, such is the throng of stout Frenchwomen in blue aprons and cloth boots promenading hatless in the hot sun, and such is their resolve not to yield an inch of the small available space. What is it on which they fatten, with an inevitability that neither hastes nor rests? Their appearance would suggest a diet of sofa cushions, stewed in lard; yet their purchases seem mainly to consist of pennyworths of radishes, bottles of claret at fourpence apiece, and yards of that crusty bread which, though it might make a very reliable walking-stick, could in no other sense be regarded as the staff of life. Whatever it may be, let us walk on the far side of the gutter, with the hand-barrow people and the dogs, that we may not be maimed for life among the cloth boots. The bakers' shops seem to have much of the custom; their big guillotine knives lop off endless yards of *pain de ménage*, and fresh supplies are introduced, carried in tall sheaves from dens at the back of the shop, while a gratifying glimpse of the family breakfast is obtained with the opening door. Here, at a shop with a fine marble counter, a fight has arisen with the suddenness of a cyclone. The customer, punching a three-*sous* loaf of brown *pain de seigle* with a cast-iron thumb, has pronounced it stale. Madame behind the counter has, with the air of a stage duchess, coldly informed Madame the customer that, on the contrary, it is perfectly fresh. On this the battle has instantly raged. The ducal calm of Madame of the shop vanishes; she is transformed into a virago of the ordinary kind, with a command of language that is less ordinary—is, in fact, incredible. The customer screams like a cockatoo, but is obviously going to be worsted, and Monsieur of the bakery has protruded his long nose and truculent moustache from the inner room. His face is in itself a breach of the peace.

In the next shop there is a great calm. It is a butcher's, and the only customer is an old woman, with a white handkerchief surmounting her corpse-white face, and a strenuous, shaking hand folding together her blue apron with its load of marketing. She is buying two *sous'* worth of soup from a vat in the back kitchen, and is complaining in a toothless lisp that she has not been given her full share of the cold grease that lies on top. Madame at the desk, a large, red woman who suggests a skinned bull-dog, does not seem aware of her presence. We find the old woman again at the vegetable shop opposite, watching with her unfaded black eyes while a penny-worth of spinach, ready cooked, is ladled on to a sheet of paper, weighed, deducted from with a dingy spoon, and handed over in its paper wrapper with the green juice dropping from the ends. Three eggs, no bigger than golf-balls, are her final purchase; one buys eggs here by their superficial area, and not according to romantic theories of the newly laid, theories that are unassailable by argument and quite unpractical. These are taken from the heap marked eighty *centimes*, and that they are sold for five *sous* is a fact that the British mind must accept, but may not hope to grasp. The somersault from counting by *sous* to counting by *centimes* is one of the most frequent and shattering episodes of the French market. It may happen to you to be told that of two frying-pans, one is thirty-five *centimes* and the other nine *sous*, and the process of determining which is the better bargain results in a mental paralysis that is rendered more complete by the impatience of the shopman, who has neither a kind heart nor a sense of humour.

The grocer's shop at the corner is doing a steady and arduous trade. Half its wares are outside, labelled attractively in *centimes*, and the broad blue backs of the housekeepers form a solid bulwark round them, scarcely penetrable even by the furtive and circuitous street dog. In the thronged interior may be discerned at intervals a bonnet, with plumage agitated by conversation, and by violent shocks received from convolutions in the ruck of buyers. By virtue of the compactness of trimming, and a certain cautiousness in the shade of lavender of the ribbon, it is recognisable as an English bonnet, and its wearer as one of a class whose sufferings have too long remained uncommiserated. She is one of the English mothers who have uprooted themselves from home and the tried and trusted suburban tradesmen, to live in Paris with an art-student daughter, to create for her a faint and famished semblance of the Kensington *ménage*, to endure torments of anxiety about damp linen, to nourish for the *garçon* of her hotel the strongest hatred of her life. The French of her peaceful schoolroom days has little in common with the clipped commercial slang of her uncongenial marketings, and at this moment she suffers an acute helplessness in the effort to carry out her daughter's instructions about getting back three *sous*, at least, in return for an emptied bottle of *alcool à bruler*. She can only, in compulsory dumbness, accept the fact that she receives nothing, much as she has to submit to the spectacle of Monsieur Pouradoux's tall young man

ONE OF A CLASS WHOSE SUFFER-INGS HAVE TOO LONG REMAINED UNCOMMISERATED

rooting with his fat French fingers among the strawberries she is buying. She knows that when Ethel comes back from the studio she will be displeased about the three *sous*, and she feels culpable, but above all things helpless. The workmen at a *cabaret* door call out, "Oh yess! Engleesh spokken!" as she passes with her discomfited face, and a boy thrusts into her hand a gratuitously distributed supplement of a halfpenny newspaper, with a coloured picture of a *décolletée* lady breaking open a grave. It seems to

Ethel's mother the completion of the antagonism and strangeness of all things.

The Rue de la Gaieté overflows at one end into an open-air market of vegetables and flowers, and sometimes, as to-day, of singing birds, poultry, and brooding families of cats. Should the passer-by cast so much as an eye upon these, he falls into the toils of the market-people. They press the cats to their bosoms, extolling their probity, their cleanliness, their race; each has been in its turn the happiness, the day-star, of some lonely hearth, but to Madame they will sacrifice their treasure for ten *francs*. Madame remains unmoved, and they fling aside the domestic treasures and snatch the birds out of their cages; they bring out more cages, and yet more birds. They hurl these aside in their turn, and unearth crates of seemingly moribund tortoises; so that the victim, weakened by seeing what huge trouble has been taken on her account, finally falls, and possibly embitters her future life by the purchase of a tortoise.

But at present there is immunity; the market breakfasts. A little girl of eleven, sitting alone at a table with a bottle of claret on it, turns with a bulging cheek to eulogise her chickens, but she does not follow it up. She is breakfasting and is reading her newspaper, so that business takes an inferior place. Has not a Parisian gentleman of the shop-keeping class murdered his wife, from motives of jealousy, and are not five columns of the paper devoted to it? Is not the rival most probably described as a brave or a great *garçon aux grands yeux bleus*, and his sobs recorded with a sympathetic hand? The French Ministry may change like a kaleidoscope, England and France may tread upon each other's toes in Central Africa, but these things are disposed of with a few patriotic shrieks in half a column.

Domestic Parisian crime is what the little girl and her fellow-readers require, and the supply seldom fails.

Take it all in all, it is, perhaps, the halfpenny French newspaper that is the crowning feature of the apotheosis of the *sou*.

MARTIN ROSS.

January 1895.

THE DOG FROM DOONE

IT was when I was at Sandhurst, and that is not yesterday. I was at home, in West Galway, for my first Christmas leave, and I was very much aware that it was not Holidays, or even Vacation; it was Leave. The fact was even more impressive because for others of the family, it was Christmas Holidays; for four others, to be exact; mere schoolboy brothers and cousins, and quite beneath any special notice from a Sandhurst cadet.

I arrived in a stately and fitting manner, with a gun-case and a new fashion in collars; the holiday party turned up on Christmas Eve, pallid, unwashed, still, in one case, seasick, and minus their luggage, according to immemorial custom, but none the less still eating penny-in-the-slot toffee, still reading four-penny magazines. The seasick member of the party spent his Christmas in bed, and continued to make heavy weather of it (twenty-three was the official record of catastrophes); and I think that it was at this time that the dormitory was established as a first line of supports by the Dog from Doone.

The house was full, and I was obliged to accept exile in Patmos, a room so named for simple and obvious reasons. It was at the end of a wing known as The Offices; underneath were stables and a coach-house; beside me was the chamber of Lally, the general utility man, beyond him was the schoolroom, and beyond it again was the dormitory, a large whitewashed room, into which had been cast the

57

four schoolboys. They had not seemed to have much luggage, but their dormitory had the appearance of being inhabited by four large families. The remainder of the containing capacity of the offices was in the hands of rats, and of a colony of bees that lived under the floor and crawled forth at night to see what the candle-light meant. The offices were connected with the house by a sequence of passages on the ground floor; they possessed a door into the yard, and a door to the front of the house, and they also possessed a draught, by day and night, that recalled the compressed gales of the Tube Railway Stations. The Passages were looked on as second choice by the women who came to sell chickens, and other conversationalists, first choice being, of course, the kitchen. No one could foretell the moment when their candle would be blown out in the Passages, and I was wont to traverse them at night with a bicycle-lamp.

It was on one of the wettest nights of a wet Christmas week, when the wind had the big Connemara roar in it, that I made my usual progress to dinner with the bicycle-lamp, swiftly, because I was late, and cautiously, because the worn flags were slippery with the damp that they sweated forth in such weather. In the darkest section of the Passages something rushed past me, a low, fleeing thing, on which there was no time to turn the lamp. The impression remained of a grey-and-black dog. I heard its claws scrabble on the flags as it went, like the lash of a whip, round an open door, and was swallowed up in the tremendous night. My way lay near the kitchen, and from thence there rose a female howl that would have been blood-curdling had it not turned suddenly and healthfully into a lament for " me whipped cream." Grasping the position, I uttered the classic screech of " Gone Away ! " and, in response, the cook came into action armed with the tongs, and accompanied by Lally, who was armed simply but plentifully with his own vocabulary. The least of his desires was that he might give the thief the full of the poker, the most pious of his wishes that the divil might blister and roast him, and the cook sandwiched between these efforts the long tale of the depredations, the supernatural cunning, and the mysterious omnipresence of the Dog from Doone.

Dinner was late, and there was an aching void where the whipped cream should have been; a holy war was proclaimed by the head of the house against the buccaneer, and a cartridge was vowed to him on his next manifestation. But his tactics were not perfectly understood; it was duly recognised that after a raid followed a lull, so that the invaluable element of the unexpected was maintained. His paternal home in the village of Doone knew him not; his owner was instant in promises of his execution without benefit of clergy when next visited. He had, he said, a month ago, put him in a sack and thrown him in the lake, " and the same evening what'd be shaking himself afther me up the road only me lad ! It must be he ate his way out o' the sack. But afther that he wouldn't let one in the counthry put a hand on him."

It seemed to me that a certain distrust was perhaps justifiable, in the circumstances. It was reported later that he had been seen following a cart of turf into Galway, and it was assumed that he had passed into other spheres of activity.

The bad weather that began with Christmas did not cease during Christmas week. The rain blew in from the north-west in spiky showers, and from the south-west in buckets, and went back to the north-west and began all over again. Grey pools stood in the fields, ditches turned to ponds, bohireens into running brooks, and the language of the people who could not shoot was quite out-classed by that of the people at the other side of the country who could not hunt. Such weather had not been seen for forty years, they said, not since the time the hounds came up this side, because the Master had made a bet that he could find and hunt a fox in West Galway. He won his bet, but he lost some of his best hounds, drowned in flooded bog-holes. When he returned, that which he said did not tend to the renown of West Galway.

On the last night of the year, I lighted my bicycle-lamp at 1 a.m. with the intention of going to bed. Bridge had prevailed, and a solemn whisky and soda had been drunk all round in honour of the New Year; I yawned excruciatingly as I traversed the Passages. It was here that I heard a dull crash, somewhere ahead and above, followed by the thump of running feet, accompanied with vague sounds of battle. These things were not outside my experience at Sandhurst and elsewhere; I ascended the staircase without unnecessary parade, and, had I not stumbled on a rat-eaten step, might have made a sensational entrance to the Dormitory. When I recovered my-self, dead silence prevailed; I opened the door and found complete darkness and deathful stillness before me. In the four beds lay four sleeping figures, with the bedclothes up to their ears; on the floor was a candlestick; a chair was piled on top of a dressing-table, a curtain, a saucepan, and many other *objets d'art* were on the floor. I stood in silence, and heard convulsive breathings, as of those who have been under water; I turned back the clothes of the nearest bed, as one peels the sheet off a horse, and revealed the youngest of the schoolboys, fully dressed, and very hot indeed. The heaving of his chest suggested the finish of a quarter-mile. Beside him was a brindled dog, remotely allied to the collie, with pale eyes that reflected the grey of the hair round them. He cowered, and looked up at me as one who says, "You've got me. I'm beat. What are you going to do?"

It was the Dog from Doone, handing in his checks.

I did various things. The young gentlemen arose at my bidding from their couches and undressed, and I possessed myself of their candle, and also of a pistol (bought for one-and-eightpence from "a man" at school), with which the wardrobe had been impartially bombarded. The Dog from Doone, it was explained, only came there sometimes. He lived in the woods, on rabbits. There was an imminent tearfulness in the tones of his bedfellow. I took the purple silk cord from a dressing-gown provided for one of the party by a deluded mother, and fastened it round the dog's neck, on which he and his companions obviously gave up all for lost.

I marched him out, determined to maintain discipline in its strictest sense, and he tugged at the purple cord, in desperate efforts to bolt. I certainly was not going to admit sympathy, or tell the culprits that I had never seen a creature more heartrendingly convinced of his own superfluity and unpopularity, or felt anything more scantily covered than the bones of his shoulders under the thin grey coat.

I shut him into Patmos, and went forth with the bicycle-lamp to the kitchen. Thanks to a genial system of general confidence, I raided it and the larder with success, and annexed half a loaf of bread, a jug of milk, and a plateful of hashed mutton.

When I returned, the Dog from Doone was under the bed. It was not easy to lure him forth, even though his wolfish eyes devoured the cold hash from afar. He yielded at length, and drove his muzzle deep into it, and snatched it in gulps, with his teeth clashing on the china, looking over his shoulder for the pursuer at every moment. He had the bread and milk too, and when it was finished he was visibly recovering his belief in human nature. He was a young dog, from his fresh teeth and pink gums, and the blue-white of his eye, that showed as he watched every movement of my hand. He made up his mind at length, and came to me, and put his paws on my knee. He smelt of the woods, and the mud was caked in his hair, and he told me in his own way how frightened he had been, and how they tried to drown him, and how he only stole because he was half-starved (a statement which I only partly accepted). I made a treaty of peace with him, and he understood it all.

What I was going to say about him to the authorities I did not know; in the meantime I made a bed for him with my rug, and he accepted it, and looked me in the face as man to man. A bed, recognised and ordained, means to a dog the Franchise and the Old Age Pension all in one.

At this point I feel it to be due to myself to mention that I had had only one whisky and soda at Bridge, and none after it. I merely state that before I had got my waistcoat off the Dog from Doone arose in his bed, with his hackles up and his eyes staring. He did not growl, he only stared, at the window, as it seemed to me. He left his bed, and advanced very slowly in the same direction, and uttered a strange and dismal bark.

It was a quiet night, the quietest for a week, and

when I pulled up the blind and looked out, the stars were shining, the tree-tops were distinct against the sky, and the grass was pale against the dark barriers of the woods. Streaks and splashes of water lay in the sodden hollows of the lawn, near the house a drift of white mist was clinging to the grass. I informed myself that it must have been a cat in the passage, when the drift of mist began to move. There was no wind, yet it rose till it was like a stack of wool, it sank and spread, and it was like a flock of sheep, moving slowly past the house. The Dog from Doone barked again, a discordant, unhappy bark, ending in a hollow, howling note. When hounds are singing in kennel, one sometimes hears that note, and if we knew what hounds mean when they sing in kennel we should know a great deal. At the same moment there was a clatter in the stable below, as of a horse starting up and struggling to its feet—a peculiar sensation passed down my backbone, coupled with a strong desire to rouse Lally from his slumbers next door. I felt, however, that it might be difficult to explain the situation to Lally, and meanwhile I was plunging into a coat, and cramming on fishing boots, on top of my evening trousers. I slipped the dressing-gown rope again round the neck of the Dog from Doone, and he slid downstairs on top of my heels; his back was still up, and his eyes glowed green in the light of the bicycle-lamp. It was a highly un-pleasant manifestation. We doubled round the end of the house; there was a wide space of grass before me, backed by a wood, and crossing the grass slowly in the starlight was the flock of sheep—no—not sheep—a pack of white hounds. They went on into the wood, over a wall, and they were blurred and cloudy as they went over the wall.

I admit that from this point everything becomes

rather muzzy. I remember what the loose wall felt like when we climbed it, and how the dog and the bicycle-lamp complicated everything, but I said to myself that I wasn't going to do without either. That white, cloudy look was all through the wood, and several times I saw the white hounds in front, that I can swear, but they were always outside the light of the bicycle-lamp, no matter how I turned it. I remember standing still, with the dog trembling against my leg in a most infectious way, and my head very dizzy. That drifting white stuff made everything swim—but I had to go on. The water was in over the top of my boots, as cold as ice. Suddenly we were going down a steep bit, and I saw the hounds gliding away over a flat, open place, and then the white stuff covered it all. There were rocks, and I lumbered on to one, the fishing boots making very bad going. I was going to jump down when the Dog from Doone jerked back hard, and I lost my balance, and went down into miles of fog. Something that was alive and frightened in me said, " You're done for," and went away.

A week afterwards Lally stood at the foot of my bed and said that thanks be to the Lord Almighty, I was grand. There were bandages on my head, and it ached.

He found me as he went through the wood on his way to early Mass on the Holyday. And I might be in it now, only for the dog. Divil such yowling and barking ever he heard as what was in the wood, and it in the one place always, and what did he get in it only myself, and the back of my poll cracked on the rock, and the dog minding me, and a puce sthring out of his neck. And what signified only the shwallow-hole that was before me, and it able to take a rick of turf with the flood that was in it—" It's what the people say, that any dog or crayture that was near dhrowned, like that fella, have great understanding afther. And in any case, if there was a person that had a half glass taken, and he not to be used to it, he might see many a quare thing out before him in the woods, and that's the dog that would know it. Sure, the man that owned him had a shebeen." It may have been the desire of Lally to minimise the supernatural, it was also possible that it was his candid conviction. In either case to argue the point was of no avail.

The Dog from Doone was lying on my bed. I looked at him and he at me, as man to man. He rolled over, showing a sleek side. He was at peace with all men in an understanding quite outside the sphere of Lally or men of the shebeen.

MARTIN ROSS.

F

WATERS OF BABYLON

PERHAPS it was some vagrant geniality of spring in the veins, perhaps it was merely the moral feebleness remaining after influenza. The tradition that it is a kindness to see people off on journeys rose up in youth and freshness, a slight thrill answered to the thought of watching for the first time an ocean steamer move forth in huge composure to the East; ultimately a hansom clapped its doors upon me, and the flap in the roof fell on the name of Liverpool Street.

Victoria Street, grey as lead even in the most golden day of summer, was a tank full of thick air; Westminster loomed with blurred outlines; then the Embankment, and some semblance of clearness and distance; Cleopatra's Needle, pale and slender, spoke as in a dream of Egyptian deserts and horizons thick with heat, but the river at its foot was pitted with rain, and the roar of Big Ben to it was sombre as the voice of John Knox preaching before the Queen of Scots. Ludgate Hill; Threadneedle Street: a dirty ant-heap, where the two-legged black ants sped to and fro in their appalling uniformity; the buses jammed and strove, uniform, too, in purpose, in freight, in the hideous ease of the conductor's repartee. Monotony and strife and gloom; a delirium of similarities in black cloth and preposterous headgear; those may be envied who leave it for countries where life, however acute, must fall into step with the Eastern cadence, must go in colours and doze in the heat.

Liverpool Street station knows neither heat nor doze; scarce, on such a day as this, distinguishes between day and night. The faces of the travellers by the boat-train were careworn in its yellow half-light, anxious and confused as they searched at the bookstall for such works as seemed to combine length and staying power with the least possible tax on the intellect; their figures advanced or dwindled in the nauseous perspective of the platform, urgent to the last, driven by the unseen stress of departure. A group, scarcely less than criminal, cheered as the train moved out into the rain, and thereby placed, as Mr. Kipling has said, the " gilded roof " on what was without it a moment of sufficient fiasco. A bad cheer is a worse thing than even bad champagne, and has in it the same hollow festivity, the same prevision of regret. Out over the wet roofs of White-chapel glided the train, a sullen, squalid outlook for eyes of farewell; brown wastes followed, seemingly composed of ash-heaps, Apocalyptic in desolation, oozing malign juices into slits that ran starkly into an *ewigkeit* of fog. At some unknown limit of the wilderness, the train stopped among houses and shops, a place where goblin children leaned against the greasy lintels of the public-house, watching with eyes of subtlety and weariness the pageant of the street. Eventually, beyond further wastes, mis-shapen warehouses alternated with the light scaf-folding of masts and yards, and we came to a standstill beside a shed. It was the Albert Dock station, the Gateway of the East, the threshold of England; apart from these titles it was a barn of entirely simple conception, capacious, doubtless water-tight, and almost too unambitious to be called repulsive. From it swarmed a smart gang of natives in white trousers and brilliant colours, and fell upon the luggage;

they were like supers in some grimy pantomime,
their bright frippery was hateful in the rain, their
eyes had the cold Eastern lore, the occultness nur-
tured in a separate life, on meditations for ever
untranslatable.

The side of the steamer was like a black wall, the
gangway steep and shelterless. Why should gang-
ways be shelterless? Why should anything in these
concentrated, costly efforts of civilisation be uncom-
fortable and rough? The decks were very wet. A
wind from the dim and ruffled river bullied the little
curtains that draped the entrances to the deck cabins;
down in the saloon was all the painting, the gilding,
the upholstery that mask the inexorable exigencies
of ship life. The next century will surely be sorry
for us, and talk about survival of the fittest, when
they contemplate our ideas of ocean travelling at its
best; the draughts, the awkward staircases, the
depressing utility that lurks, iron-handed, in the
velvets, the cramped affectation of reckless luxury,
the irrepressible sense of making the best of a bad
business. A ship is, indeed, a primitive thing for
this age of history, with its paltry brag against the
elements, its groaning thraldom to them; ironclad
or ocean greyhound is but a brilliant makeshift, a
vain thing to save a man, and an adept at making
him miserable.

A long brown Lascar went past under soaked
awnings; he trod deftly, he swung his legs forward,
as a tiger's hind-legs swing, with strange inertness
of the shoulders, with feline litheness about the
muscles of the back. He was strikingly picturesque,
inimitably Eastern; but none the less the desire for
foreign lands was fizzling to its conclusion, and
giving place to a self-congratulation that was worth
many desires. The shore bell clanged a note of

release, and caused an access of activity in the dismal rout of passengers, Gladstone bags, gaudy turbans, muddy white trousers, and brown shanks; farewells drew to their acutest, and were cleft in twain at the gangway-head; then the lull and relaxation of the empty railway carriage, the abiding sense that the thing was done, that it had been a mistake, that it would never be attempted again.

Yet it had its compensations. The Apocalyptic desert of ashpits now possessed beauties of the soul, Whitechapel became the threshold of home, Liverpool Street had undreamed-of welcome beneath its roof-tree. Hot roast beef and Yorkshire pudding were the most immediate outlet of patriotism; how un-saloon-like were the lofty proportions of the refreshment-room, how fresh-complexioned the waiter; how friendly, subsequently, seemed the buses, how national the hansoms, how maternal, how immutable, the Strand.

MARTIN ROSS.

1895.

IN THE FIGHTING-LINE

THERE was a moment of hot lull in the debate. We had delivered ourselves of the particular argument that a week of canvassing had proved to be the most telling, and our pulses throbbed with our own eloquence. The stalwart old farmer, who had sat silent in the corner, stirred in his chair, and said, " Wot I says is, 'e that believeth and is baptised, shall be saved, and 'e that believeth not——"

He did not flinch from the conclusion, and neither then nor since have we been able to discover any connection between what he said and the subject under discussion. He wielded the tremendous text as easily as one of his own pitchforks, and his wife groaned, with a perfunctory religious ardour. By an inner current of sympathy we knew that she yearned for our departure in order that she might clear away the tea-things that stood on the table; but the heart of the canvasser must be steeled against such perceptions.

Over against us sat the farmer's son, a clerk-like and self-satisfied youth in blue serge and spectacles; on the plate in front of him were the bacon-parings of his evening meal, out of his mouth proceeded bigotry, ignorance, and the Gospel. The room was perfectly clean, and the boarded floor had a bit of carpet on it; the farmer's wife had, among other things, taught her men to wipe their feet, and purity of political motive seemed inseparable from such white-washed walls. The very growth of the roses outside

OTHER AND BETTER-KNOWN COTTAGES

in the sunshine was clean and free. The young man did not know how they and all things fell into keeping with his arrogant independence, how they made melancholy the memory of other and better-known cottages, with the hens on the floor, and the calf in the corner, and, for the cultured growth of the roses, the wild tangle of the briar, the idle glory of the golden ragwort.

The political discussion wore on to its close, with fair hearing, with arguments from father and son, bewildering in their remoteness from the point at issue, with the vials of the Revelation emptied irrelevantly forth in chapter and verse, with that ready belief in an opponent's honesty that makes the strength and the weakness of England.

The old farmer heaved himself on to his legs to see us to the garden gate, the socialistic son pressed tracts into our hands, the tired pony of the canvasser was turned for home, and the clatter of the tea-things told that the arrested activities of the housewife had been resumed. The heat, that had been stupefying throughout the fervent day, lingered in the roads and hedgerows; clean women, with pale, respectable faces, sat among the flowers at the cottage doors and breathed the warm breeze; the Conservative blue or the Liberal orange placarded the windows that their hands had made so bright, but there, it appeared, their political opinions found their single outlet. They regarded with pessimistic resignation the preoccupation of their lords with these matters, the blue or the orange, Colonel Jones or Mr. Smith. Theirs it was to fill in, stitch by stitch, the political designs, sketched by Colonel Jones or Mr. Smith, and sanctioned by their lords in those long ale-house symposiums which they accepted as the inevitable vehicle of politics. Upon them, in their daily labours, fell

the ultimate burden imposed by those remote poten-
tates, the Members of Parliament; dumb as the
farm horses that toiled on the long roads, paying the
piper in unresentful effort without a thought of
calling the tune.

Till midnight voices at the archway of the hotel
debated heavily the alternate attractions set forth
by Mr. Smith and Colonel Jones : when brisk footsteps began to move again in the early morning sunshine, the names of the rival candidates were still
in the air. At seven-thirty the landlady was at my
door, with a beaming face and the *Standard*, the
latter, obviously, already read to the bone. In those
days the *Standard* had no " Woman's Page "; Suffra-
gettes, militant or otherwise, were as impossible as
aeroplanes, and Suffragists crept about like mice,
within walls, only occasionally showing their noses in
a sympathetic drawing-room. Not, however, like the
way of the mouse within the wall was the path
appointed for the female canvasser by the political
organisation to which she belonged, and presently,
impelled by the hated voice of conscience, weighed
down by anxieties about the coming day, we went
forth again into the arena, as cowardly gladiators
as ever drew sword.

As we lifted the dazzling brass knocker of a semi-
detached villa, we felt that it was the flinging away
of the scabbard. Was our memory quite clear as to
the numbers of the Irish electorate? Had we forgotten the figures of the latest outrage in taxation?
Was—here the door opened—was Mr. Brown at
home?

Mr. Brown, in person, replied that he was, with an
agitation perhaps traceable to the fact that his feet
were simply attired in striped socks. He hurriedly
and noiselessly led the way to the dining-room; we

sat down, so did he. He was elderly, stout, and very untidy, his striped feet writhed bashfully away under his chair in a spiral twist like a mermaid's tail. The interrupted newspaper was clutched in a tremulous hand, and over it an eye of extreme embarrassment and unquenchable amusement peered intermittently at us.

We entered, full-sailed, on our mission, gathered impetus as the old truths were trotted out, rising even to enthusiasm as the fighting instinct woke. When we had perorated, Mr. Brown, using his newspaper as a Spanish lady uses her fan, emerged from what we believe to have been convulsions of laughter, and stated that he would probably not vote at all; that, as a matter of fact, he never did. His eye rolled with almost agonising consciousness of absurdity, whether his own or ours we could not determine. A very stern parlourmaid here entered, extracted from a coal-scuttle behind us a pair of slippers, and handed them coldly to Mr. Brown. The mermaid's tail was uncoiled, the striped socks were housed in green Brussels carpet, and Mr. Brown retired again behind the newspaper. Thus hidden, he informed us, in a series of giggles, that what we had said was very interesting, and that there was a gentleman two doors off, and another at the end of the road, who would be very glad to hear what we had to say. After this he sank again behind the newspaper, and we took our leave. To the last he was excessively friendly, and madly, mysteriously amused.

We proceeded to the house of the gentleman who lived two doors off, and endured a considerable probation on the doorstep, while that sense of taking a liberty, that is the torture of the amateur canvasser, became the only idea in the universe. The lady of the house appeared; her step was noiseless as Mr. Brown's,

by reason of a debased variety of tennis shoes, noiseless as those of the avenging deities, who are shod
with felt; to our feverish eye her hand seemed to
be broad and flat from long chastisement of the
young. She regarded us and our bundle of pamphlets
with a strange, uncertain friendliness, and informed
us that her husband was up at Mr. Smith's Committee Room, adding that an agent's work was very
trying in this 'ot weather. Mr. Smith was not the
candidate in whose cause our conscience had driven
us to take the field, and the gentleman whom Mr.
Brown had sent us to convert was his agent.

Our most immediate instinct was flight, our second
was to go back to say a few words to Mr. Brown,
whose sense of humour was obviously of a robust and
practical type; finally we said we would go to Mr.
Smith's Committee Rooms, and make inquiries about
the other gentleman at the end of the road whom we
had been advised to visit. When, subsequently, we
found that he also was one of Mr. Smith's agents,
we were compelled to a grudging admiration for Mr.
Brown. Determined to emulate in some humble
degree his peculiar form of humour, we conferred upon
the agent's wife a bundle of anti-Smith literature, and
retired in the direction smilingly indicated by her.
The door did not close; we glanced back through the
railings, and saw the agent's wife in the act of opening
the pamphlets and discovering therein the cloven
hoof. It was a recompense for many days of toil.

Throughout the remainder of that long and blazing
day, dining-rooms and drawing-rooms, offices and
consulting-rooms were our portion. The wax flower
and the glass shade heard our mature opinions about
the state of Ireland, our valuable views as to the most
crying needs of the Empire. It is painful to have to
state that in those days we were younger than we are

at present, yet the organisers of our party—a party
that, like all others in those days, would have become
hysterical at the suggestion of allowing us to vote—
had no scruples in despatching us and our playfellows
to instruct elderly professional gentlemen upon the
affairs of the nation.

The heat of a peculiarly gorgeous July was prisoned
in those snug and stereotyped sitting-rooms, it stood
in beads on the bald pates of our pupils, and the flush
of battle deepened from hour to hour in our cheeks,
till it became more and more difficult to present our
case with calm to the opponent. The consciousness
of a Bacchanalian complexion outweighs the confidence in a good cause, especially when the opponent
is, as in that campaign he frequently was, a dissenting
minister with cheeks of ascetic pallor. Somewhere in
the afternoon, when ranging in the outer suburbs, a
small shed with the opposition yellow label presented
itself to us; from within came the tapping of a shoemaker's hammer, the door stood ajar, and revealed a
slouched hat and a sardonic nose and long, curving
lips beneath its shadow. The situation was difficult
but attractive. We took up our parable with a new
zest, and the lips of the auditor stretched into a smile
of cynicism and superiority, as by clockwork the first
row of nails went into their places in the huge sole;
to the ceaseless tune of the hammer the burden of our
mission was rehearsed, and still the shoemaker smiled
to himself. He looked like a gipsy, he listened like
Mephistopheles, and he worked like a machine. We
went away and left him still hammering and smiling
malevolently. It was the last of those strenuous
unchaperoned days of canvassing. On the morrow
the voters would go to the polling-booths, and we and
our fellow-instructresses were requested to betake
ourselves to the Woman's Kingdom, our respective

homes. The tired hireling pony took us back to the inn, along the level roads of East Anglia; we packed our trunks, and wrote labels for Cork and for Galway.

It would have been as easy to foresee the motor, that was to supersede the white pony, as to dream of the gay and resolute procession of pilgrim women then marching to London over those very roads, and over many another road, not to ask for votes for others, but to demand them for themselves as their birthright.

MARTIN ROSS.

July 1913.

THE OLD STATION-MASTER[1]

THE man had for fifty years of his life been employed on a railway in the North of Ireland; for thirty of them he had been a station-master. Finally he was pensioned off by the Company, being past his work, and he and his old sister came back to Galway and lived in a cabin at the back of Ross on seven shillings a week.

The craving for his native place was stilled, or rather killed by his return; when I saw him he complained of living " in this dirty cabin," and spoke with a miserable regret of his trim station-house and his responsibilities there. His head was beginning to wander, and he sat all day by the fire in the dark cottage, still wearing the blue clothes of his better days, still retaining the brevity and self-reliance of manner inculcated by years of responsibility.

Through the open door he could see the dirty, crooked flags outside of the lintel, and a rickety wall that enclosed a few square yards of manure-heap; the hens and ducks came in and out, and vexed the dull eye accustomed to seeing things in their proper place. There were few other visitors; he had outlived the friends of his youth, he had forgotten the landmarks and the aims of village life, even his speech had the twang and sing-song of the North.

As the winter days went on his mind anchored itself more strongly to the past, and allowed the

---

[1] This sketch and the one that follows it are unfinished studies taken from one of the note-books of Martin Ross.—E. Œ. S.

present to run by, a vaguely disturbing current, but outside himself. He believed himself at length to be again a station-master, and when a cart rumbled distantly on the road below, he would start up, crying that the express was coming and that he must get the line clear. It was especially his torment that the people who passed near his cabin must be saved from the approaching train. The whistle of the genuine train, half a mile away, was for him the voice of a friend, the cry of hounds to the old hunter, and seemed to soothe rather than distress him; yet he said he did not care to go down to the station and see it. It was not difficult to imagine that the smart young station-master, full of the business of the day, would have been the bitterest sight earth could offer to the old man in the worn-out blue clothes that were all that remained of the occupation of a life. . . .

*   *   *   *   *

" THE INIMITABLE PALLOR OF FRESH WATER "

A SUBTERRANEAN CAVE AT
CLOONABINNIA

A LOW hill, covered with scrubby hazel and boulders of grey rock. Below it a bay, then a long stretch of lake ending in mountains and the western sky, the broad surface pale with the inimitable pallor of fresh water. In the side of the hill a broken tree, veiled in ivy, seemed the goal of a track that led from the road close by; following the track a low opening revealed itself by the tree, deeper darkness amid the darkness of overhanging ivy. Irregular steps, half choked in mud, led down the wide, slanting throat of the cavity, there were perhaps a dozen of them. Down on the right some more short and crooked steps led further to where water dripped and dropped in darkness, a well used by the whole neighbourhood, the women making their way down the muddy steps even in the twilight, by the knowledge born of lifelong acquaintance.

The larger cave bent away under the hill, with low gullet arching away into blackness of night. The floor was a distraction of great blocks and boulders, among which a pool or two glinted in the candlelight, a living thing lurking in this tomb of some past throe of the hill. The roof drooped lower, coated and tasselled with the soft white oozing of the limestone; the ridges of the boulders were sharp and steep, the rifts between them of uncertain depth,

G

and always in the deepest crevices the eye of the
water gleamed to the candlelight.

A WATER-BEARER

The air was dead and cold; the sense of suspended weight, of huge force, of indifference to the human creature, was oppressive. At length the opening became feasible only for a lizard or an eel, and after that for the water, moving in unimaginable stealth through the veins of the rock.

We turned and worked back towards the daylight, lost to us for some minutes; the darkness seemed desirous to keep us, and created a childish horror of its dominion.

Then the sane, firm radiance of outer day was born, the trodden grass, and the grey January sky; it seemed a new heaven and a new earth.

MARTIN ROSS.

1898.

IN THE STATE OF DENMARK

I

On an autumn Saturday evening, to be exact, in September 1893, a lodging in the neighbourhood of Sloane Street. A dusty wind shaking the foliage of the window-boxes and agitating the starched cornucopias of the lace curtain. Within, at an oval table where lately glowed the wool-mat and the shell-rose, my second cousin and I, in hats and veils, swallowing over-cooked tea and under-cooked chops, and conversing gloomily about the prevalence of cholera on the Continent; while in from the street, on the heavy air, came a hoarse shouting that silenced the elfin warble of the milkman, and announced two cases of the plague in London.

On the following Tuesday morning, a cold bright sunshine filling two French windows flung wide open; a room with two fat little beds in it; a street far below, paved with rough-hewn boulders, over which ramps with a deafening clatter a regiment of light blue and silver cavalry on heavy-crested horses; a red cathedral; a shop that describes itself as Boghandel, and a grateful remembrance of recent coffee, made as coffee is not usually made in England.

This is Denmark, the town of Aarhus in the heart of Denmark, and between Saturday night and Monday evening sprawls the journey to it.

Till to-day my second cousin and I knew between us just two things about Denmark—that it has given England the Princess of Wales [1] (an achievement

[1] This Expedition was made in the year 1893.

83

bright enough to throw other claims to distinction into the shade), and that it rivals even the county Cork in butter-making. For the encouragement of the select few whose ignorance is on a par with our own, we assert that it has other aspects.

The journey can be done in many ways. The guileless and enthusiastic commit themselves to the North Sea for thirty, for forty, for sixty hours, according to the measure of their guilelessness, and their selection of Hull, Grimsby, Harwich, or other bases of operation. Good sailors do the same, but they do not seem to abound on these routes. It is certain, however, that whoever goes to Copenhagen from England must go down to the sea in ships, three several times—if the ferry of Frederica be counted, as I undoubtedly do—unless, indeed, he sail direct to Copenhagen without setting foot on dry land, which is a thing done by Royal families for the mortification of the flesh. My cousin has always professed a Viking appetite for the North Sea and the sixty hours' voyage, but I cannot deny that in this instance she considered my arguments in favour of a tamer route with more than her usual impartiality.

Liverpool Street is a gloomy portal for a holiday, especially when entered at night out of the sombre and teeming city streets. The dirty, scurrying crowd of foreigners, anarchistical in appearance, with baggage of a character that makes the fellow-traveller grateful that there is so little of it, gives a foretaste of the Continent that is not appetising. It can even be horrible. Take, for instance, an episode of the last five minutes before the departure of the eight o'clock boat-train on that September night. A pallid young German Jew in a frock-coat staggered along the platform with an infinitely more pallid woman in his arms, and calling "Fader! Fader! Help!"

transferred his burden to a fat man, who had been preparing one side of our carriage as a bed, and the invalid was placed on it. She seemed crippled or mysteriously ill, and lay moaning and weeping in her place. Two very stout, dirty, young German ladies pressed into the carriage after her, and, also weeping, covered her with rugs and shawls of evil odour. The young man in the frock-coat said farewell to her and to his father, hysterically, with embraces and inarticulate German endearments; so, with the lesser fervour of an English daughter-in-law, did his wife. It was intensely painful, and the other occupants of the carriage looked out of the window, and longed for the train to start. When it did, the invalid drew her shawl over her corpse-like face and wept yet more pitiably; her daughters held her hands, they took off her boots, her stockings, they opened a band-box, and from among many details of the toilet they took cold sausages, cheese, pastry, and plums, and prepared a meal. The invalid partook of all of these and was comforted. They all partook, and the fellow-travellers averted their eyes, opened the ventilators, and endured till Harwich. Possibly the invalid and her party got no farther that night; certainly they did not enter the train that was waiting at the little station in the fresh, brilliant morning, when we stepped ashore at the Hook of Holland landing-stage. It was as well. The early Dutch sunshine was very searching, so was the breeze that was crisping the blue water of the dykes, and that slight inward misgiving that follows even a calm night on the steamer might have turned to serious qualm had the assiduous daughters with the greasy locks once more opened the bandbox in our proximity.

The corridor-train glides in a few hours across the flatness of Holland, that flatness whose absolute negation is more assertive than most mountain scenery. England does not know how to be thoroughly flat. Sooner or later it undulates irresolutely but fatally, and misses, in its efforts to be picturesque, the perfected distinction of Holland, with its enormous skies, and horizons below which the arms of the windmills sink at last like the sails of a ship at sea. All day long we strove to the north, through the immeasurable dulness of Germany, and it was past ten o'clock when the train raced into Hamburg, seeming to travel along dark causeways with, on either side, uncertain spaces of water, where the reflections of many lights writhed slow and malign. This black, light-spangled city, that we were hurrying to through the long thunder of the bridge, was the capital of the kingdom of cholera, and eyeing with disfavour the Elbe's oily waves, we decided not to eat bread or drink coffee till we were north of Altona.

Of the two women who ground at the mill, which had the better fate, she who was taken or she who was left? I hold the latter, my cousin the former; and though she was the one who was left, I now think sometimes that she was right. This is an allegory, but the facts follow.

The official mind of Liverpool Street does not encourage half measures in the matter of the registration of luggage. It says, unfalteringly as Oliver Cromwell, " Hell or Connaught," Hamburg or Copenhagen. Our plan of travel forced upon us the first of these alternatives, and our baggage was booked to Hamburg. Now we had been strictly charged by many authorities that we should not leave our train—the through train for Denmark—at Hamburg, but it was certain that the baggage must be claimed there. I was conscious of great inward proficiency in the declension of German adjectives, but could not feel this to be a moment for display, and permitted my cousin to go for the luggage with the fat porter, in the interchange of the grosser commonplaces of the language. There was a long delay. I began to be exceedingly sleepy, and then became aware of a very gentle movement on the part of the train. I assumed one of those slight passages of coquetry with trucks, by means of which trains while away the time, but I was anxious. In a few minutes the train was proceeding at full pace, and I was realising that my cousin was left behind with the tickets in her pocket. I next realised that she had all the money with her, with the exception of a three-penny bit and a halfpenny stamp. After this I remained in a species of swoon, with the dew standing on my brow, and the train rattled apace into the un-known. That there was a second Hamburg station, at which the train paused for a few moments, was almost unnoticed by me. In the absolute collapse of the future one fact remained solid, that to go to Den-mark it was necessary to change at Altona; but for this I should doubtless have burst into insane laughter and jibbering in explaining the position to the other occupant of the carriage, a black-bearded German. In this undertaking the declension of adjectives was not as invaluable as might have been expected. An ad-jective is a showy thing, but without a noun it does not materially advance the conversation; in fact I would have given away every adjective in the language for a few naked substantives, or for a certainty as to whether *wechseln* or *wachsen* was the equivalent of the verb " to change." The German was not amused, not even when I spoke of my cousin as " *meine Freund.*" He explained without emotion that the person described as the female he-friend would follow to Altona, and would have many trains for the purpose. In fact he was sympathetic in his difficult Ollendorfian

way, but by the time that his black beard ceased to
wag directions at me from the window of the train,
as it left me on the Altona platform, I had no doubt
that violent abuse in English is a more useful and
comfortable thing than sympathy tendered in German.

It was then half-past ten o'clock. At eleven the
situation had been grasped by the Altona officials,
one and all of whom accepted the fact of my female
he-friend without a stagger. They assured me that
all would yet be well; but 11.30 arrived, so did several
local trains from Hamburg, and so did not my cousin.
I sat in the vast refreshment-room among companies
of people who ate and drank heavily; their faces
looked paled and nightmarish; they seemed uncountable, and appallingly indifferent to the dilemma,
as they flocked in and out. I held on to my dressing-
bag as the one link with previous existence, and
thought wildly of the English Consul; of telegraphing
I had many times thought, but a threepenny bit
does not lend itself to such a purpose. Had an
official come in and assured me that I really did not
exist in Altona, and that I should presently find myself
sleep-walking in Galway, I should have believed him,
so little individuality has the ordinary human being
when torn from its accustomed surroundings. The
official came, but it was to beckon me forth to a private
room in the station, where a large, stern man sat before
a machine that clicked. He did not speak, but taking
from the table strip after strip of paper, began to read
along their length in the voice of the ghost in *Hamlet*.
I felt it to be appropriate. In these fateful accents he
proclaimed to me my story, told by my cousin at
Hamburg, how an English lady, without tickets,
money, or German speech, was possibly at Altona, or
possibly far on her way to Denmark. I found the
description pathetic, and realised that if I had shed

tears throughout the difficulty it would have been advantageous, and what might have been expected. After this Hamlet's father relapsed into clicking for some time, and I sat in stupor in the warm room, content to think that a connection had been established. It may have been half an hour, but at length the

"THE DANISH TRAIN HAS GONE!"

ghost opened a cavern in its beard, and said on low D in the bass : " *Sie kommt doch !* "

It was past midnight when my cousin and I met, and morning was well advanced before a doubtful repose was found between the suffocating feather bags that posed as bedclothes in the hotel nearest to the station.

My cousin's moving adventures must now be briefly recited. Her fat porter unfolded slowly—she said he did everything slowly—into a dotard of the deepest dye. After incredible dallyings in the registration department, he reappeared, to inform her that the Danish train had gone, and that her sole chance was to drive to the other station—the Klosterthor—and intercept it there. This she did, much maddened by the refusal of the cabman to start till he had received his fare. But the Danish train had long since left the Klosterthor. It was suggested to her that the other lady might have got out at the original station—the Dammthor—on finding the train about to start, and might even now be waiting there. The suggestion and the name of the station alike commended themselves to my cousin in her then frame of mind, and she caused herself to be driven back to the station with the name that seemed to her so appropriate.

The Dammthor was a desert. Not even the dotard remained, to be spoken to after his deservings; and my cousin ran to and fro like a lost soul in the Inferno, and found nothing but locked doors and emptiness. An official was at last vouchsafed from darkness, who took her to the telegraph-office, and there, as I have told, the connection was re-established. It was at about this stage of the proceedings that she was informed by the telegraph-office that unless she hurried back to the Klosterthor she would miss the last train for Altona, and when for the third time she adventured forth, she became gradually aware that all the *wagens* had retired for the night. At this culminating blow my second cousin abandoned herself for a brief period to despair, while she drifted, rudderless, about the great empty *platz* in search of a guide. But presently meeting a stout *Fräulein*, and inquiring

SHE DRIFTED, RUDDERLESS

of her the way, she found that their destinations coincided, and together they traversed the town. My cousin says that the *Fräulein* was most sympathetic, and gave her much delightful information about the cholera; but, from hints that she let fall as to the speed at which the transit was made, it seems probable that the stout *Fräulein* returned to her family in much the condition, mental and physical, of a horse who has been spirited out of his stable and ridden all night by a witch.

II

Of Altona no impressions remain but of a sunny morning, a dirty waiter, of coffee and rolls eaten with an unquiet eye on the station clock opposite, and a secret anxiety as to whether the coffee had been made with Elbe water, and, in the moment of departure, of the red cap, yellow beard, and congratulatory grin of the official to whom I had clung with the most limpet tenacity in last night's desperation, and on whom I had lavished enough execrable German to have supplied a Hamburg comic paper with jokes for a month. Then followed the swarthy plains of Northern Germany, the huge and dowdy wilderness of Schleswig-Holstein, and hourly the atmosphere seemed cooler, the sun's rays whiter. Schleswig-Holstein is not the subject that one selects before all others in talking to Danes, but indeed in any company I should find my own grave as cheerful a subject for conversation as those dire leagues of ugliness. That Germany should by force of arms have snatched it from Denmark, and that the Danes should romantically repine the theft to this hour, may be comprehended by the light of the saying that a man is never really in love till he is in love with a plain woman. The Danes say that Germany will keep its promise of giving back part of Schleswig; the Germans say nothing, and Schleswig remains the Promised Land, a Canaan with a platter face and a dingy complexion.

At Flensburg came the dismal ceremonies of the frontier: the long wait at a barrier in a draught flavoured with chloride of lime, the alien fingers of the official burrowing in tea-gown or clean shirt, then the hard-earned chalk-mark, and the freedom of Denmark conferred. Almost instantly the face of the country changed, the long, laborious heavings of Schleswig ceased, and a landscape of small, pleasant things sprang up, in which were beech-woods, and the whitewashed gables of churches, and little brisk towns with a good deal of red about them, and blue and silver soldiers. Even the railway carriages had a gayer air. The Damen Koupee was a salon, with arm-chair upholstered in a refined drab damask, and the royal monogram floated and sank in elusive silhouette among the windy billowing of the curtains, in token of State ownership. At Fredericia was the first sample of a Danish luncheon, spread at immense length in a very clean refreshment-room with a boarded floor scrubbed to a creamy white. Among the potted plants stood little bottles of claret, labelled with the choicest names of the Medoc vineyards, with prices attached which seemed startlingly disproportionate to their prestige. But no one took advantage of the sacrifice, and we discovered subsequently that no one ever does. That is to say, no one ever does twice. But everything was conspicuously clean and appetising, and the Danes ate as if they had appetites, but not with the *sauve qui peut* air which would have been inevitable elsewhere. They seem, as a nation, to have the gift of eating with calm, a simple virtue, but one denied to many of the other races of Europe.

Calm, I may add, was enforced upon me and my cousin by the extreme toughness of the veal cutlets; in fact, for half an hour or so we remained silently engaged in a process which must have given the waiters the idea that we were chewing the cud— possibly a custom with the English. Having fallen back on coffee, a second half-hour was spent in the endeavour to find out in a phrase-book the Danish for bread-and-butter, a thing which a riper knowledge has shown us does not exist in Denmark in the ready-made slice. But what, we would ask in friendliness, as man to man, what end is served by filling the phrase-book with such sentences as "The bill is reasonable," "Which is the way to the clergyman's house?" "Are the wheels greased?" "Let the boat drop down"? These are a meagre solace to the humble inquirer for bread-and-butter; indeed the remotest exigencies of life seem unable to provide the moment in which we shall find them useful. We asked in desperation for *smorbrod*, and were presented with plates covered with thin slices of cheese and cold sausage, and after a pantomime of dissatisfaction, were offered yet more plates with thin slices of beef and ham. We then left and took our tickets for Aarhus.

The burden of the tourist is much eased in Denmark by the fact that no one expects him to know anything of Danish pronunciation or Danish geography; the Danes themselves say that no one will learn their language, and therefore they must learn every one else's. They are not pained when they have to inform strangers that Aarhus is pronounced "Orhoose," or that it is, after Copenhagen, the most considerable town of their country, or even that it exists. They are humble about themselves, almost distressingly so, and generally convey the idea that it is far from enjoyable to be a little nation among big nations, revolting as the sentiment may seem to the Home Ruler.

It was two or three hours' rail to Aarhus, travelling north along the east coast, through the small, pretty country. The low beech-woods rustled on the slopes in a sea-breeze so cool that we closed the windows; the foliage was hardly thinned as yet, hardly a leaf was yellow, but autumn had irrevocably chilled the air, in spite of sunshine on the blue Baltic, in spite of pleasure-boats in the harbour of Veile, in spite of the summer clothes of the people at the stations. It was evident that this was Danish hot weather, a fact which was seriously depressing. It was a companion disappointment to discover in the countrified groups at the stations nothing of dress or face that was national or even new; the difficulty was to imagine one's self out of England. Any English market town could have supplied the clean old women with shabby black dresses and heavy baskets, the fair-complexioned schoolgirls, the tradesman's wife and her bugled bonnet, the sallow spinster, redolent of her dairy and her bunch of roses. Their eyes met ours with the wonted strangeness of fellow-travellers, and little more than that; it was the English glance, only of a more simple and friendly type, and it comprehended us by inborn kinship. But yet we wished for the foreign trick of eye, that should with lightning speed rate us as a spectacle, the slight foreign gesture that should make the cleavage of race as deep as the English Channel.

The local Danish railways seldom consider a first-class carriage to be an everyday necessity. There is a sumptuous second-class, frequented by the class known in Ireland as " high ginthry "; and there is a clean but rigorous third, also largely frequented by the " high ginthry," but the first-class is reserved for some more stately destiny. Danish ladies have very sound ideas on these subjects, as indeed on most subjects connected with money-spending, and many whose rank in their own land is too exalted for ordinary English comprehension, sit in the third-class Damen Koupee among the market women as a matter of course. Having come from a country of grosser conventions, these things were not as yet understood by us, and we did not realise the distinction of our position in the second-class saloon carriage, not even when at Aarhus Station the porters of three different hotels seemed to mistake us for long-expected members of the Royal Family. They were not stridently assertive, they were reverently assiduous—almost devout, but none of their caps bore the name that had been impressed upon us as the one thing desirable or even possible. We said, with the frigid brevity of the old *noblesse*, " Hotel d'Angleterre." They smiled and burst into oratory that might have been persuasive had it not been in Danish. We replied, " Hotel d'Angleterre," with the air of those not accustomed to waste words on the *canaille*. They again perorated in Danish, and it became disastrously apparent that there was no Hotel d'Angleterre, with which discovery we sank into disordered dispute, and the hotel porters mitigated the situation with smiles just sufficiently intelligent, just sufficiently discreet. When, a quarter of an hour later, we climbed four flights of carpetless, well-scrubbed stairs in the Skandinavien Hotel, it was hard to remember what quality it was that had made one smile pre-eminent among three, or whether the choice owed anything to the curve of supplication in the knees of the Skandinavien 'bus horse.

It is a strange thing to arrive in a town at six o'clock on a sunny afternoon and find that every human being has dined, and is beginning to think, without aversion, of supper. But anything we wished we could have, so Mr. Georg Jörgensen, the landlord, said, in such English as may be acquired from the efforts of English tourists to speak in German. He was tall, fair, and gravely polite, but seemed pre-occupied, and was almost invariably to be found with his ear to the telephone in the coffee-room, which indeed was a species of telephone exchange.

As we sat there, men wandered casually in—men who might one and all have been English, but for a certain glassy exuberance of turned-down collar, a certain tapey wildness of tie, and addressed them-selves to the mouthpiece of the telephone with the word "*hah-lo*," pronounced very softly and without a shade of expression. Among them the landlord went and came and said *hahlo*, but always with preoccupation.

At seven o'clock, while we yet sat over the coffee, the slices of black bread, and the slices of cold tongue that had followed on stewed wild-hen, Herr Jörgen-sen flung apart the curtains of a doorway and disclosed the preparations for a banquet, sparkling down a long room under the electric light. At every second place lay a bouquet, in orderly alternation with green glasses full of toothpicks; and, while we stared, a highly-scented gentleman in a dress-coat, faultless shirt-front, and grey trousers, passed us by, and placed at the head of the table a bouquet double the size of the others. A touch of humorous protective-ness in the waiter's address sufficiently indicated the bridegroom, and then the curtains were closed again.

H

Herr Jörgensen let fall the mouthpiece of the telephone and strode from the room. Had the cake miscarried? or had he miscalculated the number of toothpicks? We knew not; but the larger cause, at least, of his preoccupation was sufficiently explained. A banquet at the profane hour of 7.30 is not an everyday affair in Aarhus.

III

One after another next morning the reserves were called out. The inhabitants of Aarhus might face the east wind with low-necked dresses of summer material, but the air that mounted the stairs across the scrubbing-brush of the Zimmer Mädchen, when we emerged from the deceitful sunshine of our room, sent us back again to order out the forlorn hope of astrakhan and winter stockings.

And yet it was summer, by every vow that summer knows how to make: by glowing blue sky, by strong sunlight and deep shade, by cheap flowers and cheaper fruit, by the barren gleam of black lead on the closed jaws of the stoves. Our noses might be red and our faces blue, but the children sat bare-legged and bare-armed in the dust, enjoying themselves with every appearance of warmth; and young ladies of fashionable appearance walked about in coats whose low-cut collars were filled by a triangle of unsheltered chest and a coral necklace.

There is a river in Aarhus which looks like a canal, or perhaps it is a canal and looks like a river; whichever it may be, it is the salvation of an otherwise dry and angular town. Shaded by neat young limes, it bears in brimming silence its sluggish green burden of water to the harbour, reflecting crooked houses, loungers on the low foot-bridges, and boats of savage

red and green. Its course is draped by the gloomy
flauntings of old-clothes shops, where the children
sit in their thousands on the doorsteps and loll their
white heads among trousers at two *kröner,* and cotton
stockings at thirty *öre,* while smells unutterable rise
from the apparent cleanliness of the street.

Presently the street turns into a pier, forming one
side of a large, deserted harbour. There is one ship
alongside, discharging a cargo of indigo which has
stained the clear sea-water with a scum of furious
blue. There is a suggestion of foreign traffic about
the indigo that is out of keeping with the provincial
calm of the harbour; one feels it ought to have been
hay. Outside is a huge expanse of sea, with distant
low islands; nothing indeed is high except the red
spire of the Aarhus Cathedral, which stands with
astonishing significance on these long levels of the
coast.

The sun was almost hot in the open square by the
cathedral, and the quiet was unbroken except by
two old women in wooden shoes clattering laboriously
over the monster blocks of the pavement. Approaching from the distance was a solitary figure wearing a
poke-bonnet with a scarlet bow in it. She was
instantly discordant; even her scarlet bow was a
pert retort to the mellow brick-red of the cathedral.
She developed into a Hallelujah Lass with a pale
face, and eyes worthy of a purified soul, and we
retired into the cathedral more than usually silenced
by the energies and the anomalies of the Salvation
Army.

The swing-door slammed jealously behind us, and
we and a misanthropic female verger were left alone
in the paleness and coolness, with golden altar decorations gleaming far off behind the cobweb-ironwork of
the rood screen. Probably any properly educated

persons would have expected to find crucifixes and
candlesticks and vases of flowers in a Lutheran
Church, but we did not. We should have thought
they would have made Luther turn in his grave, not
having comprehended the strange compound of ritual
and dissent which bears his name. The cathedral
was a large, light, lofty place, with faded frescoes
and memorial paintings, and bas-reliefs of departed
citizens and their wives and families framed in a
genial decorative design of skulls. High up in a side
aisle hung a ship, floating full-sailed among the
columns in the serene quiet—the commemoration of
some signal deliverance from the sea.

From a chapel or space behind the altar came a
faint murmur of voices, steady and business-like;
we crept nearer to listen, and suddenly a chorus of
boys' voices, accompanied by one bass, began to sing
Luther's hymn—

" Ein fester Burg ist unser Gott."

It was shrilly and drawlingly sung, but the stalwart
tune shaped itself forth to completion in unavoidable
nobility, and left the arches ringing. A class of boys,
dressed in decorous black, straggled out into the side
aisle, and went scrambling and tumbling through a
low doorway into the outer sunshine. They seemed
to have instilled their youth into the torpid theology
of the sixteenth century; it sat easily on them, as
easily as Luther's hymn had been carried on their
voices.

The eyes of the female verger followed us with
misanthropic suspicion; she must be worn out by
misanthropically suspecting visitors, and never de-
tecting a crime. Why not gratify the expectation
of her life and damage a bas-relief with an umbrella,
and fly? The impulse evaporated with reluctance,

such pressure on the brain does sight-seeing induce in those by nature unfitted for it.

But the cathedral imparted solidity to our conversation during the anxieties of a visit which a lady to whom we had been given an introduction received from us that afternoon. Being, after the manner of the Danes, cultured in the language and literature of other countries, she talked to us in English of our standard classics, of modern novels, both the less and the greater, of English politics and forms of government, till we were as grasshoppers before her. Her generous certainty that these subjects were to us the mere A B C of everyday life was in itself a shelter, but we did not lose a moment in escaping to topics in which ignorance might grope for the wall at noonday and not be ashamed.

" Aarhus——? Oh yes." Our hostess' tone was one of affectionate apology. It was an old town, but not venerable; it was prosperous, but not robustly or assertively so. The Danes had not much enterprise nowadays, in spite of their Viking lineage. Would we not take off our hats?

It was obvious that we should have done this at the beginning of affairs, but being oppressed by the thought of veils, of hatpins, of the generally downtrodden appearance of the hair when a hat is taken off, and, most of all, by the implication that we were going to settle seriously down to waste our hostess' time, it seemed better to go away. In spite of much hospitable remonstrance we did so, possessors of one sinister fact of Danish life, that in making an afternoon call the first duty is to take off the hat, no matter with what expenditure of patience and back-glasses it has been put on.

At noon next day two chestnut horses, with hollow backs, ponderous crests, and faces of gentle human gravity, took us along in a barouche, against a dusty wind, at a dignified four miles an hour. The beech-woods of Marselisborg undulated mildly in front of us; the villa of the leading doctor beheld our progress from behind its rose-bushes. It was a day of solemn, comfortable sightseeing, under the direction of our hostess of yesterday, who shrank from none of the duties that had been thrust upon her. A farm-gate led us into a road between stubble-fields; then with a plunge we were out of the sunshine, and into the darkness of the woods. Beech trees everywhere, vista on vista of grey stems, slender and bare, standing upon a level floor of dead leaves. Their green canopy was spread high above; they supported it in multitudes, but without crowding, each at its proper interval. The barouche rolled smoothly on, the wheels snapped a dead twig here and there, the big hoofs of the chestnuts beat pleasantly on the earthy track, and turn after turn showed more and more beech trees. But among them not one bulky, free-grown trunk, with branches swung low and wide; nothing but this academy of pallid striplings, who yet had not the air of youth. It is thus with the Danish beech-woods, as far as we have seen them; they are close and clannish, too well-drilled to permit of character in the individual, but refined, and not wanting in a lofty sentiment peculiar to themselves and to their nationality.

Getting out of the barouche, we walked, by winding paths, to a knob of high ground, from which the trees had fallen back with true Danish respect for anything of the nature of a hill. Many feet had worn away the grass down to the pale, sandy soil, till the knob looked like a bald head; scraps of paper testified to the picnic party, and the sea, glittering to us across the tops of the trees, indicated that this was a place from which tourists should observe the view. Beech-leaves and water shimmered with a myriad flicker, and the wind was warm. When we came down from the knob, it was through the interlacing branches of hazel and sapling ash, fresh and supple as in July, and the grass was deep and fragrant. It was a moment of expansion in the half-forgotten ease of summer, one of the last of such moments that we were to know.

The sun struck hotly on the white strand where we finally bestowed ourselves, and the wall of beech-woods at our back kept out the wind. Brilliant pebbles lay around, blue and yellow, pink and grey, and warm to the touch, and the long shore stretched its curve to where the town of Aarhus lay, dull red, about its dull-red cathedral spire. All was repose and mellow colour, and the Baltic lapped upon its pebbles as meditatively as a lake. How was it that the flavour of foreign lands was wanting in it all? It was truly the Baltic of the Vikings, the Denmark of Mrs. Markham's history, but it did not feel like it; the failure may have been in our perception, but it seemed a mild, unhistoric land, where most things were familiar.

In half an hour the chestnuts took us again with immense clatter through Aarhus and its small, stiff suburbs to Ris Skov, a place of further beech-woods, a bandstand, and a restaurant. In the latter a regiment could have dined with ease—its lofty roof would have mellowed the brassiest harmonies of the band—and it was our fate to dine there, in unbroken solitude, at four o'clock of the afternoon. The rising wind moaned about the windows, and shook the trees into fretful gusts, while we went slowly through five or six courses of intrinsic excellence, cooked to perfection. It was oppressive to feel the entire skill and assiduity of the establishment brought to bear on one poor party of three, who did not even take wine. It was almost awful to see the *omelettes au rhum*, each borne by a separate waiter, approach processionally across the empty hall, flaming like sacrifices, towards an altar so unworthy.

THE AUDIENCE SHOWED A MARKED ATTENTIVENESS

In the woods, we were told, were the pleasure-grounds of a lunatic asylum, and when, later, we walked through them, by high-hedge paths, curiously interwoven, it was with an eye of serious speculation as to the possibilities of flight through this involuted trap before the kangaroo-leaps of the maniac. The gloomy green light, the wind in the tree-tops, were fitting accessories to a conversation that turned on lunacy and its startling prevalence in Denmark, and leaving lunacy, touched the kindred statistic that in every five Danes there is one who dies of consumption. What elements of morbidity, what demoralising expectancy of disease must lie behind the quiet Danish faces, that during two days of acquaintance with them had given an impression of exceptional serenity, of singular reasonableness.

Two bands, a military and a municipal, played in an open space in the wood, sheltered by the swaying beech-trees, and from the town came some carriage-loads of people to listen, and to have tea and sugary cakes in the verandah of the restaurant, and at small tables promiscuously grouped among the trees. It was the last band-playing of the year, and the audience showed a marked attentiveness to Wagner and Strauss, Rossini and Mozart, played with a sentiment, a comprehension, that may or may not have been enhanced by a sense of farewell.

IV

" *Omelettes aux fines herbes*," said my cousin, pausing between each word so that it might fall with dewdrop limpidity upon the intelligence of the waiter. Perhaps his intelligence had already done its utmost during a conversation which had walked like a pesti-lence through the German language in the endeavour to describe a penny roll; at all events, when break-fast, on its manifold little dishes, was placed on the table, it was accompanied by an omelette whose sides oozed hot strawberry jam at every crevice, and the penny rolls themselves were represented by two lardy cakes with sugar on the top. Having drawn a striking portrait of a penny roll on the margin of a newspaper my cousin showed it to the waiter, observing " *Brodchen-Brocass*," in the pleasing confidence that she was adding the Danish equivalent for breakfast to the German diminutive of bread. Perhaps if she had remembered that *Frokost* implied the morning meal of Denmark things might have been different; as it was, the waiter took away the sugared cakes and returned no more.

" God help thim that's sthrugglin' in foreign lands,"
as the Galway women say when their daughters go
to service in England; sweet omelettes for breakfast
and many other surprising things will be their portion.

A wind that would have done credit to March was
making life a burden to the yellow lime trees by the
canal, and it was with March's false radiance that the
sun glared in upon us while we ranged over the plates
of black bread and cold sausage and dried herrings
and whortleberry jam, and gave an intermittent
attention to the assortment of dogs dozing against

GREAT DANES

the warm wall of a sheltered alley outside, in all their
wonted sloth and self-seeking. Since arriving in
Denmark we had faithfully and trustingly waited to
see the Great Dane in his native luxuriance, as the
pet of the butcher's boy, the commonest of street
loafers, but so far he was withheld. Curs of new and
dreadful variety there were; a blend amounting
almost to a national species, of the crocodile, the
jackal, and the wool-mat, and in every street might
be encountered pugs, pale in colour, enormous in size
and dignity, and fully entitled to a special class at
any dog show, the breed to be called the Great Pug;
but there was nothing else great that we could discover. The Great Pug, however, was in himself a
satiating spectacle.

We were sorry to leave Aarhus, with its clanking troops of light blue cavalry, and its ceaseless clatter of wooden shoes over the implacable paving-stones, but our regret would have been many shades deeper had we, while there, been given anything on which to bestow our wardrobes except a long pole with a crown on the top, and had we not been required to sleep beneath billowy bags of feathers. But these things seem to be the inalienable custom of hotels in Northern Europe, and are perhaps survivals of a time when something handy for hanging scalps on was sufficient furniture for the prehistoric guest-chamber, and something speedy and simple in the way of bedclothes was essential for occasions when it became advisable to terminate the guest unostentatiously.

At twelve o'clock the low hills and the beech-woods were gradually shutting out the red roofs of Aarhus from us, as we crept south along the coast in a branch railway, and the faces of our fellow-travellers in the third-class carriage were becoming almost rigid in their unbroken gaze at us. It was not surprise—there were no prying and self-conscious side-glances; it was merely a whole-souled, full-eyed interest, as unwavering and as far removed from intentional rudeness as the gaze of dogs during afternoon tea. As, one by one, our audience and their baskets got out, and were left behind in the leisurely bustle of the little country stations, a tangible weight seemed removed from our consciousness; it even became possible to eat fat, greeny-yellow plums, embarrassingly full of juice, under the unswerving eyes of the last two market-women, a mother and daughter, stiffening as they sat through unbroken miles of silence.

The seaside village of Hou (pronounced " How,"

THE UNSWERVING EYES OF THE LAST TWO MARKET-WOMEN

with a fine simplicity) was our destination; to reach
it was indeed the final effort of the branch railway,
which there expired in a kind of lethargic despair,
among weedy grasses and sand-heaps and dogs and
children. It had the air of a settlement about its
few cottages, ranged among young pine plantations,
in dubious effort to be a street; the interrogation
that its name expressed was the perpetual sentiment
of the place, in its uncertain growth, its general isola-
tion. Everything was bending before the strong,
sandy sea-breeze, but the sea itself was strangely
calm, as if it had gained a philosophy of stillness
during centuries of the wind's oppression.

Apart from the cottages, on the edge of the soft
and quiet beach, stood a square villa, as wind-beaten
and almost as lonely as Stevenson's " Pavilion on the
Links "; and through the rustling, straining shrubs
of its pleasure-ground we came, full sail before the
wind, to the hospitable door that was waiting to give
us shelter.

The sudden repose and quiet within were almost
stunning, as was also the realisation that we were
launched irrevocably into Danish private life, and
must cope with it as best we might. More than
that, we were immediately to dine out, so our hostess
informed us in her broken English, that was so
courageous and so piquant compared with our ungainly flounderings in German. It was now three
o'clock, therefore it was time to dress for dinner.
With sinking hearts we did so, and, as well as I can
remember, it was on this occasion that we first noticed
that our hair was beginning to fall out in handfuls;
it may have been an effect of Danish air, but it was
on this afternoon of stress and brain-pressure that
it first became a prominent fact. Even the red-and-
white setter here, in spite of her good manners,

looked at us with furtive curiosity, and received both English and German blandishments at a polite distance; how much more unapproachable would be the Danish aristocracy in its mystic grades and conventions !

Grasping our evening shoes we set forth, at the hour when at home we should hardly have got up the lawn-tennis net. We were tired from a long morning and a third-class carriage; we were spiritless from want of luncheon, yet our appetites were jaded by the gingerbread biscuits and fruits of the journey; in fact, no worse contributions than we could have been offered to any dinner-party. By a short walk through clumps of young pines, and a windy struggle along a straight carriage-drive, we came to a large house, standing dignified and ornate among the roses and bright flower-beds of its pleasure-grounds; a typical foreign country villa, with all the foreign air of elegant leisure and perpetual holiday, very different from the grim practicality of so many Irish country houses, built as they are according to the primary conception that a house should be a square box, and that its architectural features should be disposed in stern imitation of the human countenance, a door in the middle with a window on each side.

Within were spacious rooms of an old-fashioned solidity and plainness that cared nothing for cheap draperies, and trusted for ornament to pictures, to splendid china, and to the throng of flowers that gave to the air the unspeakable refinement of their perfume. Coming towards us across the pale, satiny parquet, was an old lady with white hair and dark eyes and straight brows, and a welcome whose kindness and unconventionality made us aware that great ladies are of the same pattern in every country.

There were several other other guests: gentlemen in dress-
coats and grey trousers, ladies in elaborate dresses
that suggested a garden-party, but had certain hints
of evening about them; these compromises being
usual except at dinner-parties of the more majestic
kind. We were aware of the presence of a pastor,
recognisable by his dress, and of the accompanying
presence of the Fru Pastorinde, recognisable by the
mysterious similarity of clergymen's wives in all
climes, but the remainder were problems in a foreign
tongue. . All were introduced to us, and all evaporated
from our proximity like water on a hot stove, and
then folded doors were thrown open, and with the
announcement of dinner we knew that the hour of
trial had come.

Our hostess was visibly canvassing her available
men for the most suitable victims, and acute sympathy transcended amusement as we saw the candidates for the honour make polite but obviously
agonised excuses. How gladly, how gratefully, should
we have sat in respectful silence at a side-table while
these hapless strangers dined unmolested, but we
could not tell them so; we had to wait in arch expectancy till the forlorn hope was ordered out, and
a small, middle-aged gentleman with an imposing
title was introduced to my cousin with the intimation
that he spoke French, while to me was apportioned
another elder, reputed to speak a little English. At
first his English certainly amounted to very little,
and seemed almost as limited as my own supply of
German, but I presently realised that in some unfre-
quented brain recess he possessed solid blocks of the
language, and they gradually melted forth. Like
most of his race, he had an alarming knowledge of
England and its literature, combined with a depreca-
tion of his own country that may have been a wish

to be polite, but partook of that national dejection
that daily was more apparent to us. There was no
dejection, however, about the dinner-party in the
aggregate, and no doubt about the Danes being good
talkers; every tongue was going, and every face
looked bright; the pointed moustache of my cousin's
companion was twitching in the assiduity of his conversation, and she herself was evidently saying
" *Vraiment !* " with a gesture whose Parisian *abandon*
had yet in it some unconscious touch of the Skibbereen apple-woman. Dinner progressed slowly in
nearly the English rotation, but with flavours of far
more than English subtlety, and with slight yet
curiously noticeable differences of detail. The knives
and forks were massed at the right-hand side of the
plate, the glasses were ranged opposite to us on its
inner side; between and with the courses we ate new
and delicious jams with a spoon from a little plate
moored throughout near the glasses, and the vegetables and sauces were passed on from hand to hand
by the guests themselves. All, except ourselves, cut
up their food at the beginning of affairs; then, dis-
carding the knife, picked their way through it with
a fork, and with a leisurely neatness that deprived
the act of eating of much of its inherent savagery.

It was over at last, and there remained only the
feeling that I had eaten too much and not talked
enough, when every one rose, pushed their chairs in,
and began to shake hands with each other, saying
something that sounded like " *well bekommen.*"
We hoarsely murmured some similar sound as guest
after guest shook us by the hand, but what it was that
others replied to the salutation of our hostess we
could not discern, and could only gasp and grin when
our turn came. It was afterwards explained that
the mysterious sentence was " *Tak for Maal,*" a

politeness of the most elementary kind, meaning
" Thanks for a meal."

Presently we walked in the garden in the autumn
air that was a thought too autumnal, while the sea
glowed with its strong strange blue, and rose like a
hill to the horizon, and the clumps of beech-wood
looked black on the pale, flat coast. Like the drowning
man to the straw I clung to the lady of the party
who spoke most English, and in my determined
monopoly of her society, gave her, I cannot but fear,
cause to regret the accomplishment. It must have
been six o'clock when we came back to the house
and settled down in the drawing-room to serious
general conversation about Ibsen and Danish nove-
lists, to music, and to the vague business of an
evening party. Our hostess sat on a sofa behind a
round table, and talked in German and French, with
a running undercurrent of Danish, with inimitable
ease and cordiality; the men settled down to whist
in the next room, and the clock wore on to eight.
At that hour we were again summoned to the dining-
room for a large informal meal of tea and fruit, and
ethereal varieties of the Aarhus sugary cakes and
sliced cold meats; and still I clave to my English-
speaking victim, though my tongue was stiffening
from the root. Whist followed, into which my
cousin and I were imported, thereby for ever degrading
the English standard of whist in the eyes of the
Dane. Yet it was a relief to find one medium for
exchanging thought untrammelled by language; to
trump one's partner's best card and see him squirm
in instant appreciation; to revoke, and discover
malign intelligence on the face of the adversary; to
refuse to lead trumps, and realise that therein is
the touch of nature that makes the whole world kin.

It was past ten o'clock when we walked back

I

THE BEACH AT HOU

through the dark pine plantations to the Pavilion on the Links that we had left six hours before. The wind had dropped, and the sea was sucking and mouthing about the weedy beach, a low-voiced discontent in an otherwise immense stillness.

V

It might have been a spirit voice murmuring at the bedside in some language that even a dream could not assimilate for its own purposes. When my eyes opened, the delicious reek of coffee was steaming up from among various bread-and-butters and pastries on a tray, and something that sounded like " *Fairsegawd* " remained on the ear, while the door closed on the starched skirts and blushing bashfulness of the housemaid.

It was not the first time of noticing this mystic murmur. Customers in the Aarhus shops had invariably opened proceedings with it; when tendering payment they said it again; the shopman gushed it forth when he brought back the change, and with renewed unction when he handed over the parcel; railway officials and passengers said it in chorus when the tickets were snipped. Hamlet and the grave-digger must inevitably have used it in handing Yorick's skull about, but Shakespeare is slipshod in these matters. It is spelled " *ver saa god*," and signifies primarily " be so good," but life seems to hold no possibility in which it is *de trop*. It cannot be reduced to a system; it must be used with a large blind confidence, like a patent medicine.

I do not wish to make reflections on any one's capacity for sitting "foot to foot " with the aristocracy, but it is a remarkable fact that on the morning after our first dinner-party my cousin breakfasted on effervescing caffeine and lavender salts, and was not seen till eleven o'clock *frokost,* when she toyed with something kippered, with wan and exaggerated cheerfulness. Half an hour afterwards we were out in the wind again—a wind that made our clothes bear the same relation to our bodies that the flag does to the flagstaff in half a gale, and it may be added that the flag was generally half-mast high. The beach seemed immeasurably long and desert-like as we strolled along it through coarse, sparse grass and powdery sand, with the wind humming in our ears, and the sun staring in a pale blue sky. The only sign of life was a flock of geese putting forth to sea with the pomp of a Viking fleet; the waves rocked and lifted them with an infant enthusiasm that seemed beneath the dignity of the Baltic. The wind was doing what it could to rouse the sea to a sense of its importance, but succeeded only in rousing the temper of my second cousin in exact proportion to my skirts, while she endeavoured to kodak me and the beach. I will only add that I have heard much of instantaneous photography and snapshots, but have not found anything instantaneous about the sufferings of the photographer's victim.

We were presently taken by our hostess to a *maierei,* one of the great dairy farms that make the face of Denmark drowsy with the lethargy of grazing cattle, and fill the heart of the English housekeeper with questioning as to the merits of Danish butter. Scudding before the breeze we passed through the village of Hou and the waving skirts of a beech-wood, past a ploughing-team ruling lines of brown across a boundless tract of green, trenches where a fir-wood was to be planted, and finally found a long, red-brick house, a green garden full of fruit trees, and a village of sheds and outhouses, the home of three hundred cattle and their commissariat.

All were now sprinkled abroad over their enormous pasture-lands; the big central yard was empty, and the endless rows of stalls contained nothing but cleanliness and some farm-horses, pale, serious creatures with heavy necks and hollow backs, looking as if they were fed on curds and whey. In the absence of the three hundred ladies to whom our visit was specially directed, the manager very kindly suggested that we should see the pigs, who in these dairies are largely cultivated as receptacles for skimmed milk, and we lightly acquiesced.

Nothing that we had yet met with in Denmark proved as rapidly satiating as the atmosphere of the first pig-shed. It was a long, large house, filled with pens as neatly subdivided as the squares of a chess-board, and within them lolled uncountable swine, grunting with repletion, squeaking with an ill-humour which may have been conversational or may have been merely an accompaniment to their own vile medita-tions. It was a nightmare of guileful eyes, leering up in red sockets, of carnivorous noses, snuffing with watchful greed, of an odour that paralysed feeling, appreciation, politeness, everything but the determina-tion to fly. It was some comfort to see that our hostess was already in full retreat, vanishing round the corner of a pen by the door, where a tall and bristly-maned boar surveyed his visitors with an intelligence and distaste that were more than human. Why is it said of prodigal sons that they have " gone to the dogs " ? Why not to the pigs, those original boon companions of the prodigal ? As Dahlia, the red-and-white setter, delicately sniffed the tainted gale of the pighouse, and withdrew to await her party outside, it seemed as if her only possible relation to him would

be that of a duenna of the most respectable and
fastidious kind.

There was another pighouse, with even more pigs
in it, the manager assured us, with a touching anxiety
for our happiness, and perhaps some remote remembrance of the partiality of the Irish for the pig.
Happily for us, our hostess realised that we had had
as much of the national pet as for the moment we
required, and intervened with a suggestion that we
should be shown the milk separator. We were taken
to a doorway at a refreshing distance, and going down
stone steps encountered the innocent fragrance of
fresh milk, cooled in pure vessels and airy twilight.
It was a gospel of cleanliness and perfection, and the
pig saturnalia was forgotten. In the stone chamber
below, deep stone vats held lakes of milk, and a
separator in the background occupied itself with
rivers of it. Everything was cold, enormous, and
full of milk. There was a quiet and well-oiled click
of machinery somewhere, and the thrust and return of
a steel arm were visible behind the separator, one
of the antennæ of the steam-engine that lurked in its
private den and dominated all things in the *maierei*.
Granaries, hay-lofts, or churning-houses, in every one
the same quiet pulse was beating; up in the angle
of the roof a cogged wheel was spinning apace, out in
the yard a long band ran endlessly across the sunny
square of sky.

We descended into a grey, stony place, lined with
grey stone shelves, where sat dim ranks of cheeses,
wholly occupied in decaying, one would have said at
the first gasp; "ripening," the manager explained,
with an appreciative sniff. Whatever they were
doing, we can certify that compared with them the
pigs were, as Mark Twain puts it, "just heliotrope."

Eventually, by some process as inevitable and as

unconscious of effort as the procession of the equinoxes, we found ourselves driving the manager slowly and steadily before us towards the garden with the plum trees. He submitted, he even shook the trees and gathered the shower of ripe fruit for us, and we also gathered for ourselves. It was an old garden, whose fruit trees, standing in the after-grass, were like pictures of the Garden of Eden; wandering among them, in hearing of the foreign speech that was going on behind, some sensation of entering into the inner and older life of Denmark came curiously and deliciously, and in a manner not to be acquired from milk separators. Perhaps we absorbed it with the plums.

Somewhere above our heads there was suddenly a voice, a young and fluent baritone, singing something about "Danmark, O Danmark," with careless strength. Nothing met the upward gaze but the purple plums glowing among the branches; the garden indeed was mysteriously deserted, and the voice ceased as suddenly as it began. The tail, however, of Dahlia, the red-and-white setter, was for one instant visible, vanishing into the low branches of a beech-tree, and that glimpse revealed a decorous tameness in the carriage of the tail that told of society. We penetrated the branches and found a trunk, a discovery not altogether unusual, but in this instance enhanced by the addition of a staircase that went steeply up among the manifold limbs. We followed the wary ascent of Dahlia, and at the height of two storeys came to a room with walls of growing branches and a roof of leaves, where our hostess was in the act of eating fruit and adjuring a fair-haired youth to sing again for our mystification. The youth was acquainted with one English phrase, and gallantly put it forth on being introduced; it was unfortunate that it should have been " good-bye," but the intention to say the right thing was none the less sincere.

That afternoon he and his baritone were imported to the villa, and the pleasant drawing-rooms were filled with Danish music, sung with boyish sympathy and the ease of abundant compass. The French windows stood open above the sea, where the tide lay silent against the dumb sand margin and the seaweed border; the wind had fallen again to a mere eavesdropping about the doorways, and the melodies rose up incarnate against the listening Baltic. It was a more peaceable music than the Norwegian, and partook a little of the national despondency, but the northern virility was in it, a directness born of power and unshaken by its own tears. The aching patriotism of a beaten country may hide itself in philosophy or resignation, but its music will tell of the wounded spirit that cannot be healed, and when Danish music is combined with a recent study of Danish history, it can make mere Irish visitors into partisans and sympathisers of quite singular fervour and futility.

At eight o'clock next morning we were on our way to church, that is to say, we were picking our way among the rusty rails and heaps of coal at the terminus of the branch railway, and dodging the engine in its rambles among the grassy sidings. Church was at Odder, two or three stations off across the prairie pastures, a clean, quiet town, or rather an immensely long stretch of paved road, bordered by villas with gardens full of ripe fruit, and by excessively respectable shops with a remarkable prevalence of photographers. It is said to be the longest street in Denmark, and after walking over its stupendous pavement in patent-leather shoes for some twenty minutes the statement seemed reliable. The white tower of the church was visible afar, topped with a steep red roof and quaint with stepped gables. Tall trees clustered about it, and gave the simplicity that belongs to the combination of white walls and green foliage. Under the trees was the churchyard, an unpretending and beautifully-tended place, where every grave was a flower-bed, in perfect order and bloom; on a child's headstone a white dove was perched with so brooding and tender a droop of the neck towards the grave that it seemed alive and grieving. The people walked and talked among the flowers and crosses in Sunday clothes of the English fashion, which is the ideal of Danish dress; yet a certain redundance of trimming and fancifulness of design showed the ineradicable underlying difference. It was all very accustomed and respectable, and the church itself had features with which Irish churchgoers are not unfamiliar: the toweringly lofty pulpit, the high, narrow pews, the conversational cheerfulness of the congregation in the interval before the service, the fact that just half of those present sat with their backs to the altar. The architecture was heavy, of the squat Gothic kind, and white- and bluewash prevailed; the gorgeous tomb of a noble family glorified one transept, an organ gallery filled another, and in a low alcove was an ornate altar, with two massive candles, and a reredos of white carving on a blue ground. The pews were as narrow as wagonettes, and in each two rows of people sat face to face and foot to foot in a manner that almost precluded the possibility of kneeling. As no one made the attempt it did not seem to matter. A species of clerk took his place at the altar rails, and immediately the officiating clergyman walked up the aisle in a black gown with a white ruff round his neck, and bowed and nodded as he came to his more intimate friends in the congregation. Standing with his face to the altar, he read many Danish prayers and collects, to all of which

the clerk said " *Ammon* " loudly, while the audience
sat erect in a silence which might be supposed to
imply consent. Activity became at length noticeable

THE PREACHER

in the organ gallery opposite, a hymn was given out,
and a man silhouetted against the window behind the
organ took hold of a handle and began to make backward dives, as if bathing from the end of a rope.
The organist, with a histrionic swing of a somewhat

mop-like head, began to declaim a long and pompous tune; the congregation took it up with a startling burst into existence, but remained seated. The Danish hymn-books naturally gave no clue to its significance, and even the tune, which might have possessed some dignified nationality, was so long-drawn-out as to be meaningless. It was indeed amazingly slow, loud, and dogmatic, and the organist swung to and fro in sympathy with the lagging rhythm, and the organ-blower dived with increasing *abandon*, and the old men around us soared to the high notes, or their vicinity, like sopranos.

There followed more prayers and more hymns, and the preacher ascended his high pulpit and read the Creed, recognisable by its metre and by the notable fact that the congregation rose and joined in it. The sermon was a well-gestured piece of oratory, and the preacher's face was picturesque and Elizabethan in its setting of white ruff; he was listened to with flattering attention, except for a little boy, who yawned lamentably, and went through long wriggling contests with his guardian, and one of the dotard sopranos, who devoted himself to a minute and distressing toilet of the face and whiskers, on a principle borrowed from the household cat.

One would say that the Danes must impose a strong reserve on their public religious feeling. They say of themselves that they are not eminently devout, and indeed their service does not tend that way, mixed as it is of cold conventions of ritual and the even colder independence of the congregation. Yet the reserve of religious feeling must be somewhere; it must be more than a frigid consent that has preserved the unimpeached Protestantism of Scandinavia.

VI

A September morning spent in the fair of Galway
proved to be no sort of preparation for the September
morning spent a twelvemonth later in the fair of Odder.
I thought that the two might have had some points
in common; that the aboriginal Danish peasant
would arise out of his fastness, like the " mountainy
man " of Connemara, who drives shaggy cattle and
ponies from untold distances, and finds the dark hours
of plodding a mere whet for the day's enjoyment, for
the long, luxurious lying, the intense moment when
the lump of mud, long flourished in the air, is at length
flung upon the back of the wild-eyed heifer in token
of purchase, the reeking jostle in the public-house,
the dripping can of XX, the glasses of whisky, the
green apples.

But if Denmark, in all its pasture and sand, yet
conceals a fastness, the aboriginal Dane does not come
forth from it to the fair of Odder. On a slope outside
the town two lines of booths and a hundred yards of
trodden grass made a street, where a clean and quiet
crowd moved to and fro, pleasantly, but without
humour, and inspected gymnasts, monstrosities, and
merry-go-rounds with complete intelligence and un-
altered suavity. At the end of the street was an
equally quiet gathering of horses and cattle, through
which moved the peasant buyers and a prosperous
dealer or two, conducting bargains with an absence of
histrionic display, and an indifference to the artistic
aspects of a lie, that verged on cheerlessness.

The horses were of the unvarying Danish breed,
long in the back, high and massive in the quarters
and crest, with the faces of placid and serious human
beings; the cattle were religious in character, and a
singular contrast to the nimble and free-thinking herds

THE FAIR OF ODDER

of Galway. Yet if the raw eccentricities of the live
stock, and the lavish intellectual display of the Connemara man were absent, so also the English prosperity
and robust arrogance of merit were not salient in
beast or owner. All was rational, respectable, more
by effort than by easy circumstances, void of extremes,
and singularly void of humour.

In long refreshment tents the farmers sat in decorous
rows at their dinners; a few wore high-crowned cloth
caps of an unfamiliar shape; a few had the broad light
beard and square shoulders and sea-blue eyes of their
Viking ancestry; but the majority were men of middle
height, with pale faces, irregular noses, and light,
reasonable eyes, full of acquaintance with civilisation.
To find refuge from one of many showers, my cousin
and I paid our thirty *öre* each, and squeezed into an
acrobat's tent, where three fair-haired children in dirty
tights went gravely through a succession of somersaults and contortions, while the big drops drummed
on the canvas overhead, and the wet Danes crowded
in behind with unceasing pressure, and the anxious
faces of the little acrobats called forth applause for
each elementary achievement and time-honoured pose.

Having escaped in a fine interval from the yellow
glare of the wet canvas and the carpet of damp grass
in the tent, and made a tour of the booths, we bought
confectionery from the banks of it that sloped solidly
upwards to the chins of the old women who stood
behind the counters. For fifty *öre* we received an
amount that would have wrecked any English nursery,
and having sacrificed our hostess' children to the
necessity of getting rid of it, we forthwith became a
prey to misgiving. It was reassuring to find them
presently revolving with hideous velocity on the backs
of a giraffe and a tiger, to the unexpected strains of
" Patrick's Day." It occurred to us that Nature had

possibly pointed out the antidote, and that even the so-called merry-go-round may have its base uses. Looking back to it all, we cannot help feeling sorry that we did not patronise the Chicago Exposition. It was there, in a very large tent, presided over by a young lady, whose severely English tie and high collar were mitigated by an eruptive burst of paste brooches. No one, so far as we were aware, set foot in the Chicago Exposition throughout the long day, not even a tentative inquiry disturbed the frozen sulk of the doorkeeper.

After the crowding and staring of the fair, the sticky mud, the showers pattering on an acre of umbrellas, it was an act of singular repose to get rid of wet wraps in the hall of a villa that stood back among its fruit trees by the street of Odder, and sit at a flowery table, eating pears and plums and grapes, and drinking the delicious Denmark coffee. Cream-coloured Tauchnitz volumes lay about the tables, and the talk went easily to and fro among them and their authors, none the less easily, and all the more pointedly, because of the Danish accent and the earnest choice of English; the air breathed of the impalpable foreign elegance, and all things were suave, simple and characteristic. For the twentieth time the foreign gift of conversation impressed upon us our own inferiority; it was impossible not to suffer in self-esteem from contact with that graciousness that thinks it worth while to decorate slight things, that pliant responsiveness that accepts the proffered idea as an acquisition, and returns it whetted and burnished like a borrowed lance. Not in the casual villa of the British Isles is the art of talking thus usually demonstrated; how infinitely more probable are the sodden generalities upon life's dullest details, he inevitable climatic convention, the caution that is swept away in a burst of confidence about the cook. Certainly in Denmark our only assurance of the cook's existence was in her cooking, which in itself was eloquence.

Presently there arrived a landau, sent for us by our hostess' brother, the magnate of the district, head of the great house of Holstein-Rathlou, and holder of the hereditary office of Hofjägermester, a position corresponding in some degree to that of our Master of the Buckhounds. The landau had two tall carriage-horses of the English pattern, between whose ears glittered the curious ornaments, like tiny gongs suspended in toy stirrups, that are worn only by the horses of the nobility in Denmark; the coachman had a gold band round his hat, and wore a long moustache (the latter in strict accord with the Danish fashion for servants). We, and our friends of the morning, took our places, and were driven swiftly and softly through the woods of Rathlousdahl. We went by thickly-shaded tracks, with sideward glimpses of open country that revealed tall trees drawn up in line along straight roads, and cattle grazing on boundary-less pastures; now and then a herd of fallow deer would flit spectrally across an upland, leap into sil-houette on its crest, and drop out of sight behind it. It was a wood of free and various growth, interpreting in a thousand transparent tints of green and filtered lights the gleam of afternoon sun that was shining among the wet leaves, while the springs of the landau bounded soothingly with the occasional rut in the deep sand of the track, and the horses went with complete kindliness up and down steep and crooked places and over unparapeted rustic bridges, while the twigs brushed their unresenting ears, and the coach-man and his hat bowed as incessantly as Royalties to escape destruction.

Ibsen was the topic that grew and prospered in the pleasant atmosphere; a fruitful topic at all times in Denmark, and sure to be treated there with a sanity and a temperateness born, it must be, of innate knowledge of Ibsen's country, his language, his people, frequently of Ibsen himself. He does not seem to startle these neighbours of his; they appreciate strongly, they condemn vigorously, but there is no discordant outcry of tongues newly versed in Ibsenese, no fever and jerk of initiation, no enthusiastic flourishing of new brooms. There appears little attempt to claim for him a meaning beyond the simple reproduction of character and action; he himself claims no more than this, and would not, so we were told, support in any way the theories of those who will not leave unexpounded even the dolls of the Master-Builder's wife.

It was natural that Ibsen's women should induce comparison with Englishwomen, who, perhaps by their own fault, seem so badly understood by the foreigner, so insulated into a theory. It was not, of course, their shortcomings of which we heard most, yet some slight consciousness of reservation, hardly amounting to disparagement, made us glad we were Irish. There is nothing aggressively superior about being Irish—at least, other people do not think so, and however that may be, there is a sense of kinship between the Irish and those who are not English that is curious, yet unmistakable. Taking this into consideration, we ventured to hope that it was intended as a compliment when we were assured that we were quite unlike the English, but it was not altogether so gratifying to discover subsequently that Englishwomen were specially remarkable for their rich and handsome clothes.

The discovery was present with us as the horses took us along the main road again, and dived in at the

K

Rathlousdahl arched gateway in a manner that did credit to the official with the moustache. Two or three clanging seconds in the tunnel of the archway brought us into a large square courtyard, with a fountain in the middle of it, and buildings of mellow brick all round. The carriage drew up at a flight of steps, and a most splendid person, with a long black beard and glittering buttons, let down the step and tendered an obsequious arm.

We were presently in a long, low hall, poising ourselves with infinite caution on a mirror-like parquet, while our hostess, the Hofjägermesterinde—which signifies Chief Court Huntress—welcomed us to Rathlousdahl in English as fluent as our own. Through an uncertain number of darkly picturesque reception-rooms we went forth to the gardens, where, in a space among immense trees, was a lawn-tennis ground, a sight that we in our ignorance had expected as little as a snipe-bog. A game was going on, and the Tower of Babel sensation was again uppermost as the English terms " Sairve," " A-Lett," " H'out ! " came to us like rays of light out of the weltering chaos of Danish. We took our turn, and cannot confidently feel that we upheld the athletic reputation of our country, even though one opponent was a gentleman in jack-boots, and the general tendency was to sink all party feeling in order to keep the ball going as long as possible. Later we walked in the park among the great beech and horse-chestnut trees, and noted the cunning of the Danish landscape gardening in every wooded rise and sequestered pool. A quiet pleasure-ground in the shelter of a hill was guarded by two bronze dogs, modelled with astonishing vigour by the great Polish sculptor Jerichau, father of our hostess, the Hofjäger-mesterinde. The rich red brick and thatched roof of the servants' wing of Rathlousdahl bounded one long side of a seemingly boundless kitchen garden. Quaint windows peered between the laden boughs of fruit trees, many-coloured pigeons wheeled and stooped over the low roof, and the clanking of horses' hoofs on the pavement of the courtyards on the farther side had a mediæval sound that harmonised well with the old-world beauty of the garden. Rathlousdahl is a typical Danish house of the old *régime*. Great in extent, as architecturally simple as a farmhouse, its innocence of fortifications or defences speaks of an unruffled and fearless past, and tells of the mutual confidence that some years ago found practical expression in the regiment of volunteers that followed the late Hofjägermester against the Germans.

Dinner at seven o'clock felt sinfully fashionable after the homely 4.30 to which we had become accustomed. The daylight had faded out by six o'clock, and the crushed contents of our Gladstone bag renewed their youth in the merciful *couleur de rose* of shaded lamps. Some twenty guests were assembled in the central *salon*, a large, delightful room, full of half-seen beauties of carved oak, painting, and rare china. There was no calculated disorder of arrangement, such as distresses the honest furniture of many a drawing-room; everything was placed with full appreciation of its merit and a due appreciation of the comfortable. On a table at my elbow a collection of old silver vinaigrettes glittered in manifold twists and knobs; most of them had belonged to former ladies of Rathlousdahl, and had a coronet for a lid; some carried a lock of hair set in their ornamentation. Romance of a forgotten age was among them, faint and quaint as their own fragrance. It was broken in upon by the presentation of a tall and youthful Dane, with a face sunburned pink, and evening clothes of the English kind. From his left arm already depended a dinner-partner. He beamed upon me and held out his right; I attached myself to it, and the whole room advanced to dinner, three deep, like a figure of the Lancers.

Seldom have two more festive hours fallen to my share than those that followed. My partner remembered astonishingly well as much English as may be picked up in a month once spent at Newcastle; I remembered astonishingly badly such German as may be learned in a year from an English governess; my pendant on the other side knew only Danish; but when three people are equally penetrated by a sense of duty to their neighbour, language is a secondary matter. We presided, in triple state, at the head of the table, an honour that seemed almost excessive, till, in the calmer observation that comes with the fish, I discovered, across the piled-up fruits and flowers, our hostess sitting at the middle of one of the sides; further away I sighted my second cousin, talking to an elderly Count with a dignity but slightly marred by fish-bones, and then I was called on to bow over a glass of hock in response to the lifted glass and the bow of some one in the vicinity. The proceeding was repeated in champagne and Lafite before dinner was over, and seemed to the unaccustomed a sociable and picturesque survival, but one requiring the kind of head that grew in the last century, in the days when the copper barrel that gleamed on the sideboard did not hold too much wine for a dinner-party at Rathlousdahl.

When at last the finger-glasses with their floating marguerites came, in cool sequel to the banquet's long and strange artifice, my companion was talking English like a native, and my progress in Danish had extended to the discovery that the only means by which the foreigner can hope to pronounce it is by putting out the tongue slightly and moaning along it.

It is a practice not recommended for dinner-parties, but when the moment arrived for pushing in the chairs, and shaking hands with the fellow-guests, it enabled me to imitate with approximate success the words of friendly greeting that pass round a Danish dinner-table at the close of the meal.

VII

That friendship whose chiefest demonstration is to stay up late and pass the bottle, has been vaunted above its betters. It pales like its own candle-light before the friendship that is astir betimes on a sharp morning, disdaining, in the glow of its purpose, the mellow sloth that ripens in warm foreknowledge of the tea-tray. While we waited, in the superfluously fresh air of 8.30 a.m., for the engine to cease from its morning quadrille among the cinders and the dogs, and take us away for the last time from the windy levels of Hou, we found ourselves the objects of a general *levée ;* all our friends had come to see us off. It was hard to realise that it was but a week since we had come to the Villa Björnkjoer, and learned there what Danish kindness and hospitality could be. It was still harder to feel for how indefinite a time good-bye must needs be said, and how wholly inadequate—not to say absurd—were our endeavours to give some sort of expression to our gratitude and our regrets. The kindness received a touch of completion in the arrival of the lady who had given us our first experience of a Danish dinner-party, and had suffered with unimpaired amiability a manifestation of our powers of whist-playing. Looking back from the window of the train, her white hair, and eyes kindling with benevolence beneath level brows, made her face memorable among the other kindly ones as the last *farvel* reached our ears.

The basket of fruit and the bunches of roses that she had brought with her exhaled a perfumed companionship that was specially acceptable in the crowded Damen Koupee. It was several stations before the last market-woman had squeezed her way past us to the platform, and even then we had scarcely heart to begin upon the peaches; the moment, however, did arrive when the problem of the peachstone had to be met, in secrecy and silence, and it was not till then that we were aware of a line of faces intent upon us over the top of the partition. They were schoolgirls, full of motionless, intelligent interest; they studied us as they might have studied a railway novel, and with all due modesty, we may add that, to the best of our belief, they did not skip a word.

We were on our way to Silkeborg, a measure forced on us not only by the passionate enthusiasm of guide-books, but also by the fact that the Danish diffidence as to all things Danish vanished at the mention of Silkeborg; it was felt to be a certainty, and it needed no apologist. To get there from Hou it was necessary to change twice, and a good deal of spare time was available in which to study the sentences written for our learning by our late hostess in the end of our Murray. Written Danish has, at a first glance, an air of resembling English that is full of encouragement. The second glance faintly discomposes; is it perhaps more like German? Then some one speaks the sentence, and the brain reels; the sounds have no approximation to the written words. A Russian-speaking German, with his mouth full of hot potato, might come somewhere near it in effect; but no adventitious aid brings the ordinary foreigner within measurable distance of success. We eyed a door which bore the solemn inscription, " Gods' Expedition," and told each other that though we might think we understood it and could say it, as a matter of fact we didn't and couldn't, and yet another door still more mysteriously designated " Lill Gods' Expedition," " Lill " meant little; who were the little gods? Was this the route by which Odin and party went to Valhalla on the arrival of Saint Ansgarius (see Murray)? We afterwards found that Lill Gods' Expedition was the name they called the parcels' office, and lill gods were hand parcels, which is absurd.

After the second change the country seemed to have more richness of autumn about it, while yet it kept some lingering semblance of summer in hedges and gardens; the sun streamed upon us through the uncurtained glass with tepid amiability, and the landscape developed a suggestion of boldness in its contours as we went north-west towards the centre of Jutland, where lie the lakes and woods that make the Danish Killarney. In the early afternoon we neared Himmelbjerg, a wooded hill of five hundred feet high, that the Dane has, with unconscious pathos, styled Heaven's mountain. He has built hotels from which to gaze upon it, he has made zigzag paths by which the tourist may accomplish the ascent. Its steep bluff rises with extraordinary importance and effect at the end of a long and winding lake, and to look across the water to it while the train followed the curves of the lake shore was a refreshment to eyes accustomed during many days of journey to low and endless undulations.

The tourist yet lingered in his summer resorts; he smoked in verandahs that commanded a good view of the station; he saw his friends and their lill gods into the train with a minuteness that suggested a background of large and vacant afternoon; he pulled himself and his family on the lake with his coat on; he and the warm weather were obviously on the wane. All along the lake ran woods of fir and beech, and we joggled pleasantly through them to Silkeborg in the sunshine. Then we passed out of the woodlands across a river shadowed by the trees; a manufactory chimney rose incongruously beside it, and we were presently occupied in conversing by signs with the porter of the Dania Hotel.

With chattering teeth we were rattled and bumped in the hotel-'bus over the enormous paving-stones, and saw low, red-roofed streets lengthen behind us in prim perspective, till we crossed a wide square to the archway of the Dania. It was a very large hotel, and it did not surprise us to find that it was empty. My cousin and I seldom come short of our destiny. We come like Claudian, full of good feeling, but fraught with devastation; we sit, like Marius, among the ruins of hotel-keepers, accepting with simulated cheer the concentrated devotion of our victims. No footfall save our own traversed the parquet of the huge dining-room of the Dania; nothing except our faltering " *ver saa god* " disturbed the infinite leisure of the waiters.

It was still early in the afternoon, and we wandered down the sloping town to the river. Why not take a boat? My cousin knew how to ask for one, she said, and here were boats and boatmen idle by the dozen. She addressed herself to the nearest boatman, who stared, shook his head, and unloosed his soul in Danish, while the other boatmen seemed unreasonably amused. We passed on, and decided to walk in the woods of Nörreskov, on the hill opposite. Then, as we walked up the tidy, tourist-worn track,

my cousin remembered that she had asked the
boatman for a bath. "I want a bath. Can you
give me one ? " was what she seems to have said.

The Nörreskov woods are hilly, full of roads, of
benches placed for the due admiration of the view,
and of placards indicating the way to the benches.
We selected a placard with an inscription relating,
as far as was comprehensible, to the Queen of Denmark, and found ourselves on the highest point
available, looking abroad over a long, wooded valley,
and through it, over the lake, to Himmelbjerg. In
the deeps of the valley the river went with a long
bend from the lake to Silkeborg, and through the
bridges and pleasure-boats of the town to another
lake, set in the woodland beyond. It was not Killarney exactly, but it was an eminently graceful and
well-finished view, expansive too, and generously
wooded, and notwithstanding the coolness of the airs
that toyed with the summer's sandwich papers, we
sat long in contemplation of it. Disdaining paths,
we picked our way down the face of the height, and
came on still glades full of heather, and tracks ankle-
deep in silver sand; still descending, we struggled
through red-stemmed dogwood bushes, and all the
jungle that filled the spaces between the grey trunks
of beeches to the river brink, and found there a
beautiful tranquillity of mirrored trees making a
path to the mirrored sunset. A boat with a tall
white sail came on through the reflections like a
ghost, moving in obedience to some following breath
of the evening; she passed up the pictured sky-
track and became dark against the apricot west.

A steady, splashing sound grew audible, a sound
that had the methodical beat of commerce in it, and
heralded the advance of one of the ungainly *hjüle-
baade*, the wheel-boats, worked by hand, in which the

tourist delights to traverse the lakes. It advanced
with hideous strides of its spider legs and splay feet,
and the backs of the human motors that worked·
side by side humped in regular alternation as they
stooped with the turn of the handle. How infinitely
preferable to walk on the shore, to ride a donkey—
anything, rather than sit, like that tourist party,
behind those endlessly bowing backs and see toil
without skill repaid by mere progress and the ugly
trample of the wheels through the water. It plodded
on to the sunset, and we followed through the jungle
by the river's edge, till, beyond the bridge of Silkeborg, we reached the farther lake, and there found so
noble a pageant of sky and so perfect a sheet of
reflection that we could not but watch its fading,
whereby my cousin was led into desperate competi-
tion with Indian ink and a four-inch sketch-book
against the slow dissolution of glory. Even the
squat bathing-house, perched on straggling legs, had
its hour of sentiment, of dark, quaint individuality,
while the afterglow burned behind it, and the ripple
moved tenderly through its blunt reflection.

There was no second opinion about the beauty of
Silkeborg. There was no question either about the
Dania *table d'hôte*, eaten in vast solitude at a table
laid for forty. The soup, the partridge, the coffee,
are its best-remembered features; second only to its
excellence is the fact that the cost was one-and-
sixpence each. We went to bed in the conviction
that Denmark, and notably Silkeborg, is a place in
which to live often and die seldom.

But it was not the place to sleep. Before I had
finally lost consciousness of wooden shoes clattering
about the paved square, before the contest with the
feather-bed beneath which I lay had given place to
exhaustion, a flame of lightning and a crash of thunder

burst from the dark. In five minutes it was raining with mad fury, the wooden shoes clattered wildly towards shelter, the lightning was pink and hateful, the thunder banged and roared, and the wind came bellowing up into the tumult. Through the noise came the shiver and clink of broken glass below; the jeweller's window was blown in, a large sheet of plate glass against which we had that afternoon vainly flattened our noses in search of a characteristic Danish ornament. It was long before sleep could be found, and it was of an unsatisfactory kind, headachey from the electrified atmosphere, discontented because of the unwearied guile of the feather bag. Out of a dream where *hjüle-baades* crawled spider-like through heather came a sense of deathly chill; a hand that was weak with sleep strove to reinstate the warmth and found it not, till, groping outwards, the feather bag was encountered, couching in mountainous height at the bedside, like a bloated and malignant sheep.

The rain did not cease. In the morning the square was dim and dripping, and the gutters writhed a yellow overflow at ten miles an hour. We fell to time-tables, and found a train at 10 a.m. for Copenhagen; we caught it, no man withstanding our flight, not even the landlord, who yesterday had been a sanguine man, fertile in pleasure trips and *hjüle-baades*, full of calm confidence in his weather. They know at Silkeborg what it means when the autumn breaks up, and do not fritter a good lie on a hopeless cause. Looking back from the 'bus we saw the jeweller's window filled with soaked yellow planking; in my bedroom the landlord was already taking down the summer curtains. We hope that he will some day read the inscription in the visitors' book in which my cousin tried to record her esteem of the stewed partridges with whortleberry sauce. It may be a comfort to him.

Looking from the window of the train we saw Himmelbjerg sulkily endeavouring to hide its summit in low and drizzling clouds. The moment was ripe for departure.

VIII

The faces of the peasant-women in the third-class carriage looked pale and careworn in the light that came through a window blurred with rain. Not even the whelming of all outside interests in mild meditation on me and my cousin, not the instant friendliness in small incidents of parcels and rugs, removed the impression of hard and patient living, of untimely dying, of grief not distant. It was more than an impression; it was what we knew from the testimony of their own countrywomen. None of them were old; old women are not plenty among the peasantry of Denmark. There is little of the ripe and autumn-tinted age that is a commonplace of English life. It is a strange thing; the pastoral clean life that lacks the power to stay; the healthy work that spends the strength and gives nothing back. Somewhere in the simple Danish existence the adversary waits his time; and the time is often, and the escape seldom.

An even stranger thing was the reflection that any one of these unostentatious-looking women might at this moment occupy the position of being her own aunt. It was but lately that this possibility had dawned upon us, and we applied it incessantly to our fellow-passengers. Can it be to attain at least a brevet rank in the elder generation that the short-lived Danish women marry their uncles? To be the

wife of your mother's brother must give irrefutable
standing in family life. It must even lend equality
to an argument with your grandmother, inflamed
though the position may otherwise be by the blend
of mother-in-law. Reason was tottering in the
attempt to enumerate the somersaults of relationship
that might be achieved by marrying one's uncle,
when Fredericia intervened, the junction for the
Copenhagen mail route.

We sought out an empty carriage in the new train,
we filled up the corners with forbidding hand-parcels,
we spread our wearing apparel on the seats, and ourselves at full length along the cushions in the semblance
of invalids. The ruse was perfectly successful. The
train moved on; my cousin opened the luncheon-
basket. She had just got the cork out of a bottle
of *soda-wand* (which in Denmark means soda-water),
when the train stopped and the door was thrown
open. A squat and ungainly steam-barge was alongside, and beyond it an arm of the sea lay blue and
sparkling in the new recovery of the day from downpour. We got on board eventually—that is all that
need be recorded—but the *soda-wand* did not.

Somewhere in the striving and the cloud of hand-
parcels remained the impression of an English voice,
the first accent of Britain heard for a fortnight. It
was asking with easy patronage whether there were
" anything to see about here." Perhaps some recent
conversations on the subject of the Englishman
abroad were fresh in our minds, but the tone caused
a sudden vivid insight into the feelings of dislike,
contempt, and respect which our countrymen inspire
in other lands; and we also felt, for the hundredth
time, the real touch of greatness that lies in the
self-esteem of the Briton.

In a rough and cheerful breeze, we and our hat-feathers accomplished the brief crossing to the Island of Fyen, and afterwards for two hours passed through its level farms; a green and quiet country, with low farmhouses lying as if asleep, and white-towered churches set in beech groves. The afternoon darkened across the pastures, and the sunset was dying on a cold and ruffled Baltic, when the train brought us to the side of yet another steamer, and we descended the abhorred staircase with the brass binding into a large cabin with electric lights, and officers in pretty uniforms eating five o'clock dinner, and smart stewards, and all that affectation of luxury that mocks the sea-sick eye. The passage from Nyborg to Korsoer is a business of an hour or more, I hardly know. It was a period in which my cousin incessantly assured me that there was no movement whatever, and I was occupied in trying not to look at anything that swung. Sometimes in winter the Great Belt has been frozen, and the passengers have been taken across on sledges, or have walked (so some one told me); and I thought many times of tramping robustly over that field of ice, instead of sitting helpless and dizzy in this swaying prison; of the wild starlight of frost, instead of this tepid atmosphere smelling of chicken.

Yet another period of train followed, that semi-torpid time of mere existence in the half-light of the carriage lamp that comes at the end of a long journey, while thunder and lightning, as of Macbeth's witches, announced to Copenhagen that we were near. Lights and water raced by, and we slid into the terminus possessed of one solitary clue to progress, the fact that a cab called itself a *droitschke*, and that the fare was seventy *öre*. There was no trouble about the *droitschke ;* it was secured, our smaller baggage was confided to it, and it then, without a cry, without a

"HELPLESS AND DIZZY IN THE SWAYING PRISON"

sign, drove away into the night. We remained in the station yard for some minutes in blank stupefaction, while *droitschkes* whirled in all directions, and the porter was not. My cousin at length addressed herself in German to two elderly officials, who seemed to rule the outer tumult, beings resembling the most ornate Dublin policemen, of towering height, and endued with such stomachic curve as is usually only beheld in light comedy. They replied unintelligibly, but with obvious kindness, and proceeded to harangue the night air majestically in Danish. Nothing happened; we wandered away into the immensities; then suddenly, from nowhere, the *droitschke*, the porter, the luggage, everything.

Copenhagen looked brilliant and idle when we emerged into it. Opposite blazed the gateway of the much-vaunted Tivoli, and a rich clash of brass music came from it across a great *platz*, where manifold trams crossed and diverged in the spurious gaiety of their coloured lamps; placards in the entrance of a big theatre announced the serpentine dance of Lottie Foy, and the whole population seemed to be abroad, moving about the roadway in throngs, as we have seen on Sunday evenings in summer the Dublin suburban street marching in its thousand variations of corner-boy, to the piping of the William O'Brien fife-and-drum band.

The *droitschke* plodded on through the crowd in the Östergade, a longer and narrower Bond-street, where, as in all Denmark, the shop floors were a few steps higher than the pavement, so that the cellars might lift their heads into daylight, and be shops, also, of scarcely inferior dignity. The heads of the people who sat in subterranean revel in the many restaurants below the street level showed dark against the white tablecloths; one suddenly realised

the point of view of a chandelier, and found it monotonous; the *droitschke* crawled into a large open
square, and meandered like a novice on a bicycle
round a central lamplit plot of shrubs. We screamed
from both windows the awful term " Hovethvagth-
gather." We had said it to him already at the
station, and believed it to be our address. The
cabman uttered what seemed to be a companion
imprecation, and pursued an uncertain course past
the imposing white façade of a building which brilliantly proclaimed itself to be the Hôtel d'Angleterre.
Then, suddenly, a quiet street of ornate houses, and
somewhere among the darkest of them, our hotel,
the private, the family, and the almost morbidly
modest in the matter of illumination.

It was in many ways a disappointment. It was
not so much the airlessness, the dark passages where
smells of cooking walked in endless procession, the
prevailing sense of a seething kitchen region barely
kept in the background, it was pre-eminently the
saloon, in which the proprietor, a hairy and sardonic
German Jew, invited us to eat our evening meal with
an offensive fluency of English. It was indeed no
less than the family sitting-room, and, too late, it was
borne in upon us that we had, like fools, rushed in
where angels would most indubitably fear to tread.
The waiter was unexpectedly resolved into the son
of the house, and pursued his studies at the table
where we sat; his father, more insidiously, developed
into a bore of a quite unsardonic kind. Greasy maps
of Copenhagen were imported by him to our table,
and spread in acute proximity to the butter, while a
finger, that was not shamed in hue by the black
bread, travelled across them in nimble exposition
of churches and palaces. The finger and the English had alike become intolerable, when the Frau

L

proprietress, redolent of onions and patchouli, and
glittering with jet, added herself and her frowsy wig
to the family circle. The powder lay in lavender
drifts upon her nose, her satin corsage creaked sump-
tuously as she sat down to join the *soirée*. It became
apparent that she also had a desire to air her English,
that, in fact, the privilege of a social evening was
to be extended to us. We retained just sufficient
presence of mind to fly before becoming hopelessly
entangled in the social evening.

It was entirely due to my cousin's belief in her
genius for locality that we did not ask for a candle,
and made our way without one upstairs, down an
ill-lighted passage, and yet another after it. My
cousin opened a door and advanced confidently into
the dark.

"The matches are——" she began. The sentence
ended in a dolorous shriek, coincident with an advance
into the heart of the washhandstand. I found the
match-box, and the long sulphurous fizzle of the
Danish match illumined wanly an upset jug, and my
cousin standing in a coursing stream of water. My
cousin, let me say in serious eulogy, is a person who
keeps her head in an emergency. With unreflecting
devotion I cast my bath towel forth upon the flood,
and did not, till later in the proceedings, realise that
the sponge so expeditiously brought to bear on the
dingy parquet by my cousin was my own.

Nor was it till the deluge had been disposed of
that we became aware of what material assistance
had been rendered by a crack between the parquet
and the hearthstone. It was first suggested to us by
a panic fear that the growing tumult in the room
below might be in some way connected with the
accident. We heard a shrill voice screaming out
something that resembled *wand*. *Wand* meant water.

What the appearance of Herr L. meant when, a moment or two later, he stood in our doorway, was a matter fraught at first with all possible anxiety and uncertainty. There was, however, a certain relief in hearing that the water had descended upon Madame's head. The shock to her constitution was probably serious, and of a nature hitherto unexperienced, but it could not be charged for in the bill.

IX

Out of a bitter wind striped with slanting showers, we sped into the Frue Kirche, dishevelled from half an hour's search for it in the muddy byways of Copenhagen, acidulated by the inadequacy of our summer Sunday clothes to a Danish September. The swing door banged behind us, and shut out the gusty street; instantly the far-off figure of Thor-

"A MATTER FRAUGHT WITH ANXIETY AND UNCERTAINTY."

waldsen's Christ enchained the eye in the dusky niche above the altar candles, leaning in its white trance of benediction. On pedestals at the sides of the church stood the companion figures of the twelve apostles, wrapped in a separate and individual exaltation. Apart from the embodied Christianity

of their presences, the building was undevotional and
gloomy, a species of modern Greek temple coloured
drab, yet impressive in largeness and due proportion,
a firm idea carried out without feebleness or excres-
cence. The red-lined stage-boxes that were fitted in
between the side pillars were tenanted only by velvet
footstools and the sumptuous Prayer Books of State
officials, a sparse congregation speckled the free seats,
and during the period of waiting for the service
to begin, conversation went briskly on among semi-
detached groups of acquaintances.

Without ostentation, a pastor in ordinary dress
took his place at the gate of the altar rails, and was
there joined by two gentlemen in morning clothes,
who laid upon his shoulders a black robe, and de-
spatched him to his place before the altar. The
congregation regarded the proceeding with calm
no less unbroken than that of the graven apostles
above them, and the old ladies opened their Prayer
Books and spoke in somewhat less assertive whispers.
A solitary voice was uplifted, and laboured on to
its own echo, responseless otherwise throughout the
dreary loftiness and length; then an organ rumbled
and crashed up high among the columns at the end
of the church, preliminary, one might imagine, to
some mellow harmony of skilled voices moving in
temperate concert. But a dozen female sopranos,
albeit escorted by the solitary tenor of the organist,
had little of the expected effect. They sang with
deliberate and dogmatic vigour one of the profoundly
wearying hymns that are so uncharacteristic of the
music of Denmark, and are so inevitable in Danish
churches. The choir ladies uttered slow, firm screams,
the lonely tenor clave to them unflaggingly; it
became a stupefying procession of noise, and a
tendency on the part of our next-door neighbour to

be confidential in German was an alleviation. She told us that the Pastor Preior was to preach, and instructed us in our rare good fortune in being present; she was, in fact, agreeably conversational throughout the service, and the resolution to quit the building on the first symptom of Pastor Preior's ascent to the pulpit became a two-fold impoliteness. Yet the flight was carried out, unfalteringly, and in the expansive bosom of that elderly dame the seeds of a prejudice against the English have doubtless been sown.

A cold white sun looked over the edge of the rain-cloud while we scudded towards the Kongens Ny Torv, the wide and splendid square into which the greater streets of Copenhagen empty themselves, where stand the Theatre Royal, the Hôtel d'Angle-terre, and

" THE HERR PASTOR PREIOR WILL PREACH TO-DAY ! "

many ornate buildings that might have been banks, or town halls, or flats, and were creamy-coloured and modern. Across the Kongens Ny Torv, as we emerged from the all-connecting Östergade, stretched two lines of people, gazing after a landau that had passed between them, with a broad-shouldered figure in it and a red-coated coachman on the box. It

was the Czar Alexander on his way to the Russina
church in the next street; Herr L. had forewarned
us of this, as a thing to be seen, in that hour of paternal
interest while yet the water-can was not upset, and
Madame's wig was still a crown of glory to the social
evening.   We ran open-mouthed and panting through
a quarter of a mile of straggling crowd, and were
just in time to be late.   The Czar had passed in
under the *portière* of the church, where a peal of little
bells was going stark mad, each kicking and clattering
as if dancing a hornpipe to a tune of its own, and the
red carpet was already being rolled up.   A double line
of swarthy sailors from the Czar's yacht filed into
church from their attitude of attention in the mud,
and a group of gilded beings, who might have been
field-marshals or admirals, followed with a full
appreciation of the favour they were conferring on the
crowd.   Special police and detectives were everywhere, though in *gamle Kbenhavn* they have little to
do beyond enduring the humour of the street-boys,
who unfailingly detect the detective, and impart
the discovery to the street in time-honoured witticisms.
   Since that day a greater protection has been
extended to Alexander III; he has lain in state
before his subjects with a quiet face, looking back on
death in impenetrable security, instead of the hourly
bracing of the spirit to meet it in all the poor vulner-
ability and preciousness of life.   Here, at all events,
such a glimpse as ours of his existence was a glimpse
of holiday and respite from tension.   Any day he
might have been seen in Copenhagen, escaped from
the detectives and going about the streets in trams,
or in a *droitschke* with half a dozen of his nephews and
nieces, all well furnished with toys and the delicious
Copenhagen sweetmeats.   Even the Anarchists could
hardly have wished to defraud him of such unkingly

days; and the Danes must take pleasure from the thought that so much of his rare happiness was found in their country, so much of his thwarted confidence could there expand and be satisfied.

It was not yet eleven o'clock, and we made our way in the direction of the English church, walking by an unexpected and beautifully winding little lake, the Grönningen, where the yellow foliage of tall trees was reflected in the grey, sheltered water. Above the trees was the spire of St. Alban's, lofty and slender, and wholly English in sentiment, a strange contrast to the heavily-built towers and stepped gables that we had seen for a fortnight, and to the ponderous gilt dome of the Marmor church close by. Following the curving shore the best aspects of St. Alban's were disclosed, its perfect position on a grassy brow above the water, the soft grey of its stone, the delicacy of its spire. We went in with a friendly yet flat feeling of the accustomed. It was nearly filled with English sailors and marines, their faces wearing the air of cheerful swagger and sunburned respectability that belongs inseparably to their type. The rest of the congregation was a mixture of English (of the Continental resident class) and Danes, and filled all the available seats in undecorative lines. A church-warden in a creaseless frock-coat and an obviously agitated condition of mind hovered about the foremost pew, which was empty, and was closed at each end by a silken rope. With one eye ever heedful of the door, he thrust us in among the deeply reluctant occupants of a neighbouring pew, while a surpliced choir filed into the chancel, and a monotone of an uncertain timbre was uplifted from among the harvest decorations on the prayer-desk. The choir and the monotone were going through the General Confession with some slight difference of opinion about a semitone,

"FOR THE SECOND TIME THAT MORNING WE WITHDREW."

when a rustling and a lifting of heads told that the moment for the churchwarden and the silken rope had come, and we found ourselves indulging the Princess[1] of Wales and her daughters with a stony British stare.

To feel immediately hulking, superfluous, and ill-dressed is the inevitable drawback to the æsthetic satisfaction of seeing the Princess of Wales, and those who wished to keep their minds in their Prayer Books must also have kept their eyes there. The Danish lady at my left did not, indeed, attempt to do either, but beamed with a franker admiration than we had the sincerity to display, and at long intervals asked me to find her place in an English Prayer Book with quite infantine confidence. A *soupçon* of the Danish accent lisped prettily in the chanting of the choir-boys, converting " things " to " sings " and " faith " to " face " in flute-like heterodoxy, but the harvest hymns were given with a will that drowned nationality. After the third the pangs of hunger beset us, and for the second time that morning we withdrew before the foot of the preacher had reached the pulpit steps.

But not with equal felicity. A door in the transept was temptingly near, it admitted us to a species of vestry, probably a lair of churchwardens, and neatly furnished with a table, a blotting-pad, and a tall hat, so far as the wild eye of flight could see. From this we escaped by a door with a clanking ecclesiastical latch, and went hurtling into the open air down a steep flight of steps. Here, indeed, our position became desperate. We were in a narrow paved strip between the church wall and high railings at the lake's edge; at one end was a buttress, and the conclusion of all things, at the other a space enclosed by more

---

[1] Queen Alexandra.

railing and a locked gate. It was possible to go back and walk through the church to the other door; it was possible to lurk and starve in the churchwardens' vestry till the service was over; it was possible to scale the gate in full view of the Princess of Wales' coachman. We chose the last; we were even on the verge of essaying it when a voice called hollowly to us from the arched doorway, the voice of the church-warden, and the coachman may easily have noticed that we visibly dwindled from terror as the summons reached us. To stand at bay is not a thing to be done at a moment's notice with any sort of picturesqueness, and churchwardens are of such dark and unlimited significance. He did not, however, drive us before him into church again; he silently unlocked the gate and thrust us forth, and much the worst feature of the case was that we laughed.

After this occurrence the Copenhagen Sunday, that had opened with such a burst of church-going, fell violently away from grace. There was immediately luncheon, with Heering's cherry brandy, at a boule-vard restaurant that looked like a bandstand and a bungalow, and smelt of tobacco from obvious causes, and took the *Illustrated London News*. (It is always the *Illustrated London News* in Denmark, if it is not the *Lady's Pictorial*.) Later in the day my cousin went to visit the studio of a lady artist whom she had met in Paris. I did not accompany her, and her description of the visit inclines me to congratulate myself.

Having climbed for about ten minutes up a stair-case of nightmare gloom and precipitousness, she found herself at a half-opened door, through which came a strong smell of tobacco, and presently, in response to the whackings of her umbrella, a young lady, who admitted both my cousin, and the fact that her aunt, the Fröken M., was at home, in one hospitable swing of the door.

I have been able to gather but an indefinite account of the subsequent proceedings; they seem to have involved the ecstatic recognition of my cousin by the Fröken M.—an ecstasy quite untempered by the obvious fact that she had no smallest remembrance of either her name or face—the consumption of vast quantities of cigarettes and tea in which cognac took the place of cream, an introduction to a Parisian painter of unclean aspect, eulogised by his hostess as the possessor of *un fort choli dalent*, and a discussion on Danish art, in which my cousin professes to have joined fluently, even as she participated in the other revelries. How that may be I know not, but it struck me that she neglected some very attractive items of the *ménu* at Thompsen's restaurant at dinner that evening in a way that made me fear the afternoon had told upon her.

X

Copenhagen is full of water highways and byways. Walking in the early sunshine down one of the streets the vista was suddenly blocked by the black bows of a steamer moving across it, followed by the scarlet funnels, sprayed with the salt of the Skager Rack; it was like an effect in a Drury Lane melodrama. We were at the moment impeded by a bottle of Heering's cherry brandy, bought at Heering's shop, three steps below the level of the Kongen's Ny Torv, and by two wooden trays, *echt* Danish, and of incredible cheapness, so the German-speaking Ananias at the tray-shop had told us (and we believed him through much subsequent discouragement, till con-

fronted in Skibbereen, with similar trays for sale
at a less sum). It was not easy to drive these obstruc-
tions through the populace, and the steamer, when
we came up with her, was fast to the quay, and bereft
of the brilliancy of her first appearance; leaving the
dock, we wandered by a tributary canal to where the
babel and barter of the fish-market rose from a
hundred yards of women in white sun-bonnets. They
sat on a broad pavement, by the parapet of the canal,
selling live fish out of water-tanks, an operation which
it is sufficient to see once. They flung the dripping,
flapping sole or plaice on a board, they cut its fins off
with a few sweeps of a knife, and having trimmed it
round generally, transferred it, still flapping, to the
customer's basket. In what manner they dealt with
the eels that lay in black coils in the tanks we
endeavoured not to see, and fell to photographing
the fish-wife whose business was slackest. From the
jovial *aplomb* with which she shook her fist in our faces
at the critical moment—it was clear that it was not a
first experience, yet neither she nor her fellow-butchers
were eminent in that obvious picturesqueness that
has almost vulgarised the market woman. They
wore black bombazine, linsey, or some other graceless
material, undistinguished by anything peculiar to
their country, in spite of fables about the market
women from Amager Island, and their elaborate
peasant dress, the survival of a Dutch ancestry. (I
did once meet a woman in peasant costume in a street
in Copenhagen, but I believe her to have been going
to a fancy ball.) Yet in the sunshine and the clear
air the homely blonde faces and the white bonnets
had a charm of their own, and if their dress lacked
colour, there was enough and to spare in the green
and red boats that lay in the canal below—colour in
their sunburned orange sails, colour in their cargoes

" SHE SHOOK HER FIST IN OUR FACES "

of shining apples, and its flaunting challenge made five minutes with a kodak a vanity and a humiliation.

At the other side of the canal was Thorwaldsen's Museum, a depressing piece of architecture of the nature of a mausoleum, topped by a green copper dome. Behind it were the staring ruins of a palace burnt down a few years ago; beyond these, again, a round tower with a spiral ascent coiling outside it to the summit. Catherine of Russia drove up it once in a coach and four—a hideous feat, that should have atoned for many crimes. Near it, from the Dutch Renaissance of the Exchange, rose a spire more eccentric even than the tower, and infinitely more graceful, formed of dragons, who stood on their fore-legs with their tails writhed into one slender column, and their heads ravening towards the four points of the compass. To the sepulchral museum of Thorwaldsen we addressed ourselves, and contemplated the large dingy frescoes that make its exterior ridiculous, without discovering whether the very muscular men, carrying vague blocks and bundles, were the builders of the Pyramids, or an allegorical procession of trade guilds to the shrine of Thorwaldsen. My cousin had committed herself fluently to allegory when the guide-book coldly mentioned that they represented the removal of Thorwaldsen's works to the museum. It seemed hardly the moment that one would have selected out of a lifetime, and it was painfully obvious that frescoes do not thrive in the Copenhagen climate.

We passed on into the spacious corridors and halls where the multitude of Thorwaldsen's creations is set forth, from the Lion of Lucerne, and the giant statues of Schiller and Poniatowski, to cameos, and tiny busts of ringleted ladies. He lived no more than seventy years, and yet found time to release this company of nearly five hundred from the marble. He must have begun in his cradle, while he watched his father, the ship's carpenter, carving figure-heads. Probably he cut his teeth with a chisel, and made mud gods instead of pies. The tremendous group of Christ and the Apostles, and the angel kneeling with the shell, could honourably represent the best part of a career, and yet they are but fourteen figures out of the host that stands in cold trance in the halls of the huge building. The ground-floor was portioned off into many-coloured cubicles, each with its strenuous classic hero or questionable goddess, meditating, in the singular calm of an age that wore no clothes, in the midst of a strictly respectable party of busts of gentlemen with chins propped on swaddlings of cravat, and ladies with sloping shoulders, snub noses, and ringlets, as in 1830. Halls and cubicles were traversed in solitude, unbroken except by the officials in charge—a remarkably polished body—who smiled and took off their caps to the visitors at all opportunities. One, anxious to make us feel at home, pointed out a bust of Lord Byron; another, whose good manners had yielded to exhaustion, slept profoundly in a remote cubicle, impassive beneath the menace of a nude gladiator and the mild attentiveness of a Copenhagen doctor's wife. In a quadrangle in the heart of the building is Thorwaldsen's grave, a granite frame enclosing a bed of ivy, with a mere statement of birth and death cut in the stone. Lying thus in the shadow of his accumulated honour, no more could easily be added. Yet none the less is the reticence admirable.

" They find now his art too tranquil," was how a modern Dane that afternoon put the present attitude of Denmark towards Thorwaldsen. Since the morning we had visited the enormous Museum of Northern

Antiquities (which we would fain eulogise after its deserving), and the Danske Folke Museum (from which we could, still more gladly, have abstracted wedding presents, in old furniture and silver, to have lasted for a lifetime), and Thorwaldsen was already obscured behind kitchen middens, and the evolution of the toothbrush. But his tranquillity remains in the memory as the tranquillity of superior strength; he is a Milton in sculpture removed from all heats and transitions in art.

His country's art is now in transition, not without heat; there are heretics fresh from Paris schools; there are heretics of older standing, half ready to leave Denmark because of the narrowness that they find in it, there are those to whom the Parisian greens and mauves and magentas are the sin of witchcraft; but the school of the *plein airistes* is strong in the North, and in its reliance on Nature has a special fascination for these Northerns, whose passion for Nature is a wonderful exemplification of the principle of loving one's enemies. Every summer a troop of the elect settles down upon Skagen, up at the northern point of Denmark, a village of farmhouses, on a coast half blind with drifting sand, facing the cold anger of the Skagen Rack. Its creamy sand, its great horizons, its bitter blue sea, have found fame at the hands of many good artists; the canvases of Kroyer and Johannsen and Fröken Krebs carry the prickle of the sandy wind, the smell of the harsh grass, the creaking of the battered arms of the windmills, but they give no hint of the kindnesses of life, nor do they conceal the fact that wind and sand have it all their own way there, and that Skagen is a place where the inhabitants must exhume themselves and their houses every few days if they do not wish to emerge in coming centuries as a pale Danish Pompeii.

Down in Copenhagen art schools flourish, the Government school for women, presided over by Herr Johannsen and Fröken Krebs, being a pattern to all others of its kind. Its fee is about six shillings a month, and in cases of real poverty students pay no fee whatever. The school itself is splendidly large, airy, and brilliantly clean, points which those who have worked in Paris *ateliers* will know how to appreciate. On the day on which Fröken Krebs took us into it, there were three models posing in the large room and one in a smaller room; there was certainly no stint of variety and space, and much of the work showed a truth and simplicity of colour and a strength of drawing not often found in schools of older standing. The care spent on the surroundings seemed to have its reflection in the fresh and serious faces of the students; there was none of the soulful pallor and dingy intensity familiar elsewhere as the trade-mark of that type of art student whose resolve to look unconventional is the outcome of her ingrained British love of convention, whose surroundings have just sufficient incoherence to find recognition under the greasy banner of Bohemia. Fröken Krebs alone knows what long and hardy efforts were necessary before the Government school for women was achieved; what interminable sessions of Parliament; what innumerable letters and audiences; what labyrinths of red tape. Except in later years, women have been little accounted of in Denmark; ladies were the object of that chivalry that would shield them as far as possible from earning any money for themselves, while it accepted the fact that other women worked in cellars and slept in garrets, and did the same work as men, at a lower wage. But in spite of prejudice, in spite of the vapid maxims on which women of the upper classes have been nourished,

M

there is, even in conservative Denmark, a new era coming to them, and there are women who have let the world know they can work as well as weep.

The problem of meals had begun to weigh on us a good deal. There is something especially sufficing about the wonderful Danish coffee and the rolls and butter of the little breakfast; *frokost* at twelve or one o'clock became abhorrent, yet at three, when we had arrived at an appetite, it was too late for luncheon and too early for dinner. The usual end of the matter was that at a quarter to four we stalked gauntly into Thomsen's Restaurant in the Östergade, and waited in the bitterness of starvation for the four o'clock dinner. It happened almost every day, and always the unfailing Thomsen soothed us with three courses, perfectly cooked, for the sum of one-and-twopence. The delicacy and finish of Danish cooking is only equalled by its cheapness; but the Danes sigh, and say that cheap food is the sign of a poor country. Ireland also is a poor country, and we have yet to find there the restaurant that will supply sorrel soup, fish quenelles, roast lamb, vegetables and coffee for one-and-threepence, with a big, cool room, speckless table-cloths, and waiters straight out of band-boxes. England being a rich country, it is unreasonable to hope for anything of the kind there.

It was on the evening of Thorwaldsen that we unbent ourselves by going to see *Gjen Boeurne* at the Royal Theatre, a ponderous, domed building in the Kongens Ny Torv. Strange rules prevail about the booking of places; on the day before the prices are doubled, on the morning of the performance they are fifty per cent. in excess; consequently we did not book, and went early to avoid the rush. We then discovered that the rush consisted exclusively of ourselves. In the solemn silence of the vestibule our

cloaks and hats were taken from us by several very
kind but very firm elderly gentlemen, who exacted
a penny for the attention, and we were admitted to a
perfectly empty theatre, with electric light and a
capacity to receive half Copenhagen. After a quarter
of an hour the entrance of a woman and child took
away the feeling that we were the last people left
alive in the world; others straggled in, a good
orchestra struck up, and the curtain rose upon a
party of students supping, making speeches, and
singing choruses. Being in Danish, the play progressed for us in complete mystery, as far as the plot
was concerned, but down to the last super the acting
was admirable. All went with astonishing ease and
unanimity, each minor part being given its true
value, and no more than that. We had been instructed, on very high authority, that the brothers
Emil and Olaf Poulsen, of the Danish State Theatre,
were as fine comedians as any in Europe, and when
Herr Olaf strutted in with a military frock-coat
buttoned to bursting over that curve of the lower
waistcoat that is indispensable to robust comedy,
and struck his first attitude as a *passé* lieutenant
of the Sir Lucius O'Trigger type, it was easy, even
for bewildered foreigners, to recognise a finished
craftsman. It was an old-fashioned part; it might
easily have been conventional, but Herr Poulsen
made love to the ladies, and browbeat the gentlemen, and was himself browbeaten with sincere and
irresistible humour.

After the first act we wandered forth in search of
coffee, but found only peppermint and cold water,
and returned shuddering, while the remainder of the
audience ate sandwiches that they had brought with
them. Danes can eat slices of cold meat when other
people can barely entertain the thought of an ice.

During the first act, we thought that we saw our way into the plot; during the second, we constructed one of singular ability; at the beginning of the third, we threw up the sponge, and subsided into chaos. Another student party, very determined and unanimous about something or other, melted from the stage, leaving the hero solitary, in a frock-coat and tight black trousers. To him entered, seemingly with a pain in his stomach, a bent old man. The stage immediately darkened, and the old man embarked on a long speech in rhymed verse, with frequent allusions to Jerusalem. The audience fell into appropriate gloom, and we settled that he was a Jew money-lender trying to get something on account, on the plea that he was bound by destiny to return to Jerusalem. My cousin then went to sleep. The old man continued for yet another five minutes, and left unexpectedly and tragically, having dropped a pair of shoes on the floor. The stage became inky black, cataclysms occurred in the scenery, and the lights were turned up on a drawing-room, and a supper-party which included an 1830 grandmother, Sir Lucius O'Trigger, the heroine, who had throughout the piece maintained a modest silence, and the student hero, on whose feet were the shoes left behind by the money-lender. I was inspired to suggest the Goloshes of Fortune, and a kindly neighbour informed us in German that the old man was the Wandering Jew, which seemed to her to explain all eccentricities. It transpired that by virtue of the goloshes the student was invisible, and that he was to be the means of humbling the pretensions of Sir Lucius. The party supped with the utmost realism, and fell to playing a long drawing-room game, of the nature of " A Ship came from China," but of far greater intricacy, the grandparents playing with unaffected enjoyment and agility, while the invisible student mixed in, and frightened Sir Lucius with surreptitious pinches and pokings, and kept the audience in ecstasy. The happy ending came inevitably. Sir Lucius was, to our extreme regret, expelled from the stage in a state of pulp, the student took off his goloshes and became visible, and the curtain ultimately fell on his mild embrace of the speechless heroine, and the bene-dictions of grandmamma.

The acting was, as we have said, super-excellent throughout, but oh, Mr. Archer, are these the shudder-ing realities of the grim Scandinavian drama?

We went home, and felt virtuous, but very old.

XI

It was one evening when I was surveying the street, previous to throwing the tea-leaves out of the window, that I suggested that we should try the *pension* at the corner, with the windows overlook-ing the Kongen's Ny Torv. My cousin leaned out of the window, with the shoe to which she had been applying Guiche's varnish still on her hand, and considered the matter, with gesticulations of the shoe.

Next day we went. The *pension* lady had just room for us, so she informed us in good English, and at five o'clock we climbed some thousand stairs to the room where our places had been fitted into a long dinner-table. Every one else was seated, and nibbling expectantly at their extremely handsome portions of bread; it was obvious at a glance that our country people were in the majority, and that an excessive propriety prevailed. On my left was a grey-haired lady suffering from a heavy cold, on

my cousin's right was a matron with an inky chignon
and dazzling false teeth, all about us the English
elbows were decorously close and square to the
sides, the wary English eye took note of the newcomers. Sliced ham and a smoking dish of cauliflower opened the feast, and were eaten by us with
reserve as a *hors d'œuvre ;* the other guests made the
most of their opportunities, and as the dish was
proffered to me for the second time, my grey-haired
neighbour informed me in a bronchial whisper that
there would be no more meat that day, that when
things began with ham and cauliflower every one
prepared for the worst. I felt that I had lighted
on a true friend, and continued on the ham. The
English picked at it with veiled discontent, the Danes
preserved a better cheer, and some unknown foreigners
of Jewish appearance called for wine, and became
merged in oily mirth and health-drinking. A vast
platter of boiled fish followed, excellently cooked,
and silence fell while fish-bones were being assiduously sought out. The conversation of the English
was almost exclusively of the Royal Families of
England and Russia, both of whom were then represented in Copenhagen; the intimacy displayed with
their movements, manners and motives was pheno-
menal, and even a very exclusive lady with a greenish
grey fringe, who had spoken to nobody except the
hostess, was moved to contribute some special
information between the pancakes and the dessert.
The hostess smiled unfailingly upon all, but with an
eye that communed with the servants, and foreknew
the weak places of her *ménu.* Second only to Royalty
as a topic was the cholera—the chances of encounter-
ing it in Germany, the chances of taking it if encountered, the chances of recovery if taken. The young
lady who was obviously the life and soul of the

pension had much lore on the subject, and offered quinine to a young gentleman from Bristol who seemed a recognised wit. He said he would prefer the cholera, " at which remark," as the Vicar of Wakefield says, " I thought the two Miss Flamboroughs would have died of laughing."

Still in the relish of the jest the table rose, and a social evening was entered on in the next room, on blue velvet chairs and red velvet sofas. Some one played the piano, the lady with the green fringe sat apart and played a frigid game of patience with the air of one who imparts tone, and the life and soul of the *pension* got up a round game. It prospered; a Danish youth was swept into the circle, was called " Oh, nawtay, nawtay," by his instructress, and the elderly ladies hung round in admiration. A tall Swedish girl produced some sketches; she was going south to study art; she was as pleasantly gracious as seems to be the rule with Swedes, and the elderly ladies rose like a rookery and settled down about her. They had the manners of devoted young men, and told each other in loud asides how ladylike she was, and how clever; as sketch after sketch was shown they said, " The noble river ! " " The swelling mountain ! " with a beautiful, copperplate enthusiasm. The Swedish girl became eventually involved in the round game, and the Bristol young man asked riddles, of which one remains imprinted on the memory. " If the kitchen poker were aunt by marriage to the drawing-room tongs, how many one-eyed policemen would go to a cart-load of sawdust ? " This was with some difficulty translated by the Danish young man to the Swede, who received it with a politeness that could not conceal her stupefaction. It was rivalled by ours; the fact that there was no answer just serving to restore mental balance.

Some slight court was paid to us. A Danish lady, whose daughter had recently been married, was communicative in English, according to that law of things that makes a foreign tongue so strangely beguiling to confidence. Confessing sins would be easy if one could do it in very good French; revealing the family skeleton a mere luxury if it also revealed a proper acquaintance with subjunctives. We encouraged our good dame. Yes, Anna had done well. Herr Larsen had taken a fine house in the (something that began like a mouthful of hot potato and ended in *gade*), and it had cost her a pretty penny to furnish it. Oh yes, that was, of course, the custom in Denmark, that the bride's mother should furnish a house for her son-in-law. After all, as Anna had married her father's brother, the money had not gone out of the family. We each took a long breath. It needs one to accept this feature of Danish life with calm. Anna had, it appeared, been brought up with a care that well fitted her for the important position of being her own aunt. She had spent a summer in a farmhouse, learning all details of house and dairy work, cooking and mending, and making butter with her own hands; *ja, ja*, why not?—we had expressed our unfeigned admiration of Anna—most of the Danish young ladies spent a summer in a farmhouse in order to learn these things. But Anna had not learned to ride, nor yet to play lawn tennis; Danish ladies did not care for riding, and lawn tennis was as yet seldom played. We began to think that Anna had not, on the whole, a very good time. " Ah, yes," sighed her mother, as if interpreting our silence, " I have been in England. I was a time in London staying. The English young ladies are having there so much freedom. You can row in the Thames so finely, or ride the *haute école* in Hitepark, and play your lawn tennis so sharp and hardly. But with us, not so. But Anna goes much in her kitchen. The Danish ladies go much in their kitchens."

On this pronouncement followed the intervention of an English matron, who had hitherto hovered, at some disadvantage, on the outskirts of the round game. We were not the Bristol young man, but we were capable of being properly instructed. She had lived for eighteen years in Denmark, and the Danish ladies whom *she* was accustomed to mix with did not spend their time in their kitchens. The discussion raged. We sat by and devoured yawns till it emerged somewhere near the topic of dances. " Anna ollways dance so nice." Her excellent mother beamed upon us, and we followed up the subject. A Danish ball seemed to be a somewhat serious undertaking, a slow series of dances of half an hour's duration each; with a solid hot meal somewhere in the middle of the proceedings. There is an original chief partner for every dance, but turns may be taken with sub-partners. On consideration, this arrangement seems to have many capabilities and advantages. Strangest of all, is the unwritten law that girls may not wear black ball dresses, and severest, too, in a country of fair-haired aristocrats with short purses. It was the opinion of the English matron that the Danish aristocracy had but a poor reputation for dress, whether by day- or candlelight; they copied the English, which was gratifying, but the result was not good. The Dane, upon this, played the ace of trumps, by reciting as the glass of fashion the Princess of Wales, " our *goot* Princess," she added rapturously. A Galway man has said that " if it was even two cocks you saw fighting on the road, your heart would take part with one of them." Mine took part with the Dane. My cousin assures

me that hers did the same, and also that it was I
who first yawned when the discussion oscillated back
to housekeeping. Nevertheless it was to her that
our countrywoman bade so pointedly and suddenly
a glacial good-night.

The days remaining to us were few, and Frederiksborg Castle was still unseen. Our Danish friend told
us next day that a tram would take us there; we
found one in the Kongens Ny Torv, and said " Frederiksborg " to the conductor. He nodded. How simple
were the means of transit in Copenhagen! The tram
took us by a long semi-suburban road to the gates
of a park, where nurses and children speckled the
broad walks, and placid male exponents of elegant
leisure basked in chilly gleams of sunshine.

We walked by the curving edge of a lake in which
the beech trees and the blue sky and the rustic bridge
were charmingly reflected, and by doing four miles
an hour persuaded ourselves that the weather was
warm. The trim windings of the path took us
eventually to a plateau where stood a large, old-
fashioned building, too straggling for a hospital,
but of that nature. This was Frederiksborg, that
" dream of architectural beauty " of which the guide-
books cannot say enough. We sat down to give
the beauty time to sink gradually in, and the white-
wash grew whiter, and the windows more baldly
regular, till by appealing once more to the guide-
books it was discovered that we were looking at
Frederiks*berg*, once a royal dwelling, and now a
military academy. Frederiks*borg* Castle was hours
away by rail. We wandered very disappointedly to
the edge of the terrace, and looked down upon Copenhagen, a level plain of housetops, out of which rose
conspicuously the spiral round tower, the dark dome
of the Royal Theatre and the gilt cupola of the

Marmor Church. A light smoke clouded the harbour, where lay the Danish men-of-war, and the Czar's yacht, and the Princess of Wales' yacht, and all the things that sightseers should have seen; hardly a sound of the city came to us, hardly a footfall on the terrace broke the quietness. Once, when looking down from the heights of St. Cloud upon Paris, an American girl broke the silence by saying, " Well, I call it purfeckly heedjous." We had not the pleasure of her acquaintance, but we respected her courage. Cities were not intended to be looked at from above.

There was, at all events, the Zoo somewhere in this very park. We wandered till the strange lunatic voices of wild animals and birds directed us; we paid our forty *öre*, and entered a verdant solitude, with the impossible Noah's Ark creatures pacing their enclosures and begging for buns. By two things we chiefly remember the Copenhagen Zoo—by the blessed intervention of plate-glass between the monkeys and the spectator, and by the first and last glimpse in Denmark of the Great Dane. He was there behind bars, a big and sleek and slate-coloured dog, a curiosity, like other wild animals; he whom we had believed to be the guardian and plaything of every Danish hearth.

That night the great chocolate-coloured arch of the Tivoli gate blazed above us, as we put down our fivepence apiece and passed the turnstiles. The music of different bands came through the dark, coldly rustling branches of the trees, and innumerable feet crunched the gravel. Here, we had many times been told, the King and the peasant met in equal hilarity, but at the first glance neither was visible, only old ladies in couples, small boys, family parties, more old ladies. We asked the way to the band of classical music, and were directed to a tall pavilion, with a great array of chairs and tables in front of it. A horseshoe of covered-in benches and tables enclosed these; it was late in the year for open-air music, and the audience was thinly scattered over the wilderness of chairs; we got into the most sheltered corner, and ordered coffee. The music struck richly and melodiously out into the dark, cold breeze; it was a large band and an impressive one, but its conception of classical music was ancient opera overture, and a gallop in which a delirious leading part was sustained by a toy nightingale, who flew on the crest of the stampeding phrases. Yet, except for the cold that delicately nipped the hands and feet, it was passing pleasant to sit and drink hot coffee under the lamps and the restless trees, with the music crashing and wailing, and the mild-mannered people eating sandwiches and drinking tea. A young man came up to the next table, loudly addressing as " Mawther " a lady who was so rapturously engaged in shaking hands with the waiter as not to notice his approach. He seemed to be all that was needed to complete the joy of the *rencontre*, and he and Mawther, still in cordial exchange of conversation with the waiter, settled down to cold pressed beef and an unknown syrup mixed with water; then all faces were suddenly turned upwards, as a balloon drifted up into the night across the opening in the trees, and a rush for a further view was made to the door of the enclosure, headed by a white-capped band of female cooks, who had burst forth from somewhere under the bandstand. The balloon sailed fast on the brisk wind, " a pale moth rushing to a star," or an aerial ghost flying from the lamps of Tivoli; it dwindled, and passed away towards the harbour and the Baltic.

We dawdled through the crowd to another band,

that played deafeningly inside a huge pavilion crammed with people. Hardly could the old ladies place their camp-stools, hardly the waiters find passage for the little pewter tea-pots and the sugared cakes; the intolerable strength of the music seemed to add to the crush, and we squeezed forth again, through phalanxes of fashionable young men, who stood at the door in their long-looped ties and turned-down collars, into the spaciousness of cold air, tainted with bad tobacco. The noise was hardly out of our ears before the dogmatic rhythm of dance music was launched with drum and brass from another pavilion, whose ring of coloured lamps showed fitfully through the ever-rustling beech branches. Its sides were open, and all round it ran a gangway for spectators, on which the people were clinging like bees. We waited till a fat shopkeeper and his mother got down, and clambered into their places. Holding to the rail we looked down into a swarming circle, where forty or fifty couples were revolving in a waltz—soldiers in their light blue and silver, sailors in the well-known low collar and cap, shop-boys in tall hats, students, fishermen, dancing with the blowsy fair ones of their choice. They held each other round the waists, and laughed in each other's faces, spinning, racing, jostling, reversing; and a major-domo, in the centre, directed all things. The heat came up round our faces in unpleasant wafts, and the cold air was at our backs; stiffly we got down, and thought about getting home. A lake, with limelight and a ship, did not long attract us; we stood for some time in a crowd outside an open-air theatre with a drop scene formed of a peacock, whose monster spread tail furled to slow music, and revealed a juggler and his glinting knives, and his incredible feats of balance.

Everything was fresh, ingratiating, and even, in

some unexplainable and pleasant way, a little childish; above all, it was Danish beyond imitation, and the people seem to revel in its uniqueness. We were infinitely alien in their midst, and extraordinarily remote from England. One link alone, the fellow-hatred for strong tea, still bound us to the Dane, and made England even more remote. We ordered, for the third time that evening, a hot and pallid teapotful, and felt that the heart of the Danish nation was not inaccessible to us.

XII

October rain, thick and raw, October landscape, bleared and faint, a very slow train, many little stations. In the corner of the carriage a Danish lady reading a closely-printed book, without a stir save the regular movement of her eyes. It was a cheap English edition of *Oliver Twist*, and neither the dialect of Bill Sikes nor of Fagin checked the steady progress through the pages; we asked ourselves where we should be with the *argot* of a thieves' kitchen in Hanover or Paris, and my cousin's vacant triflings with the *Galway Vindicator* seemed more than ever insular.

Hillerup, Gjentofte, and many more mild wayside stations with outrageous names passed, dripping and desolate, then Birkeröd, Lilleröd, Hilleröd; and at Hilleröd we got out. Oliver Twist and his attentive Dane passed on into the blind north, whither, had we a particle of self-respect or proper feeling, we should have pursued our course, to Elsinore and the grave of Hamlet. Any tourist can now see Hamlet's grave; Americans asked for it so untiringly that the authorities gave in and erected one, to meet a long-felt want, since when the tourist has found Shakespeare

far more convincing. We remained, however, upon
the platform at Hilleröd, where, besides ourselves,
the station-master seemed the only thing alive in
the neighbourhood. It rained excessively, and the
sheeted downpour framed in the silence beneath the
station verandah; the station-master turned away,
as one who leaves fools to their folly. We found a
droitschke outside, and cheerlessly gave the word for
Frederiksborg Castle.

With all the enthusiasm of the long unemployed,
the *droitschke* whirled into a small red town, galloped
full tilt through its crooked, empty streets, on across
a towered bridge, under a great archway, and drew
rein in the castle courtyard. The rain fell as from
a shower bath, veiling the façades of faint red brick,
the steep, grey roofs, the innumerable windows; the
droitschke drove away; the silence was monumental.
We stood beneath umbrellas in damp indecision,
while gargoyles spat contempt upon us; a human
face peered forth from a portico—a seller of photographs, watching us with wan autumnal hope. We
raised no false expectations by further dallying, but
plunged into the doorway appointed for tourists,
paid our fourpence each, and were started in the
long path, roped and flagged like a racecourse, that
shows the visitor the way round the castle. Following
the red guidance of the rope, we mounted slowly,
attentively, storey by storey, from the vast banqueting-
hall and its gold-inlaid coats-of-mail, to the vaster
Riddersal, till the magnificent doorways and ceilings,
and the pictures, and the pale, polished parquet swam
before our eyes, and admiration, however genuine,
could not but be aware of aching legs, and of the
faint yet pursuing chill of a building in which no
fire is ever lighted. Since the castle was burned down
in the winter of 1859, and the nation spent £40,000

in rebuilding it, they prefer to freeze a few attendants annually to chancing another conflagration. It is probably cheaper, and it ensures activity among the attendants, who pace assiduously in the desolate suites of rooms, with faces chilled to a dappled heliotrope.

In each storey two lines of rooms looked down on a lake, pent in woodland; the castle rose out of the water like a great ship at anchor; it seemed to drift among the ripples that broke delicately against it. Frederik II planned it in 1562, and it seems a casting away of a singularly royal residence that it should now be merely destined to undermine the constitutions of tourists as they wander, half-appreciative and wholly exhausted, through its immensities. The King of Denmark prefers the more homely Fredensborg. It is disappointing that kings should be so wanting in arrogance and so addicted to homeliness; they should be as unfalteringly regal as court cards, and should sleep on their thrones.

The ornamentation that culminated in a frenzy of barbaric colour on the ceiling of the Riddersal reappeared in more temperate cream and gold in the chapel, and glittered coldly in the sumptuous ebony and silver of the altar and pulpit. My cousin was in the act of ascending the pulpit stairs, in the belief that they led to the gallery, when a scandalised female verger intervened, and led us, an easy prey, round the blazoned coats of the Knights of the Elephant and the Grand Cross of the Dannebrog, into the royal pew with its elaborate series of sacred pictures, and finally delivered us, weakened, into the hand of her confederates, the sellers of photographs. Starvation and cold had done their work. We crawled forth from the castle, possessors of the points of view that we least wished for, and of none that we had sought. The rain had at length ceased, leaving the air foggy and still. Beyond the bridge, from beneath a group of dripping beech trees, we looked back to the dim grey-and-red castle; its many spires and dormers dreamed in the grey sky; it had all the refinement and romance of a château in a French fairy tale, and absolutely none of the stark severity that belongs by convention to Scandinavian royalty. How an impious comparison with the Kensington workhouse originated, I cannot say, but as we turned away towards the station it was present with us.

Who can hold a fire in his hand by thinking on the frosty Caucasus? The heat that rose up that night from the pit of the "*Nationale*" music-hall seemed to concentrate itself more especially in our corner box, when we remembered the damp wind that had circled in the void of Hillröd station. The theatre was as full as it could hold; top gallery and dress circle overflowing into the corridors, while the pit clattered with cups and plates in the steaming ardour of a universal high tea, and the tobacco smoke dimmed all things. Family parties of the most solid respectability sat at tables and consumed tea, cold meats and confectionery, while, on the stage, other family parties enjoyed themselves less tranquilly on tight-ropes; knockabout artistes were feverishly and desperately funny; and elderly ladies, in tights and two or three coats of paint, danced with creditable activity. If a regular attendance at music-halls is considered fast and fashionable, then, as Falstaff said, God help the wicked. We can but proffer the gilded youth our profoundest sympathy if these are a customary part of his amusements. Here, indeed, the gilded youth was in the minority. Middle-aged matrons raised placid eyes to the stage, while their

N

jaws moved in bovine mastication of stodgy sponge-cake; the topical song by the lady with flaxen hair and a cracked tenor voice was received by them as tranquilly as the sermon of the Herr Pastor last Sunday; they mellowed in the heat and cigarette smoke as peacefully as hams in a chimney. At last, while the crowd thickened, came the event of the evening, Lottie Foy and her serpentine dance. A rhythmic flicker in a night-black stage, a whirling succession of butterflies and flowers, while the lime-lights hissed their shafts of wild colour, and in the obscurity of the auditorium the volleying encores roared along the lines of glimmering, piled-up faces. After it the coarse anti-climax of gaslight, the renewed clamour of waiters and tea-things. The crowd ebbed; we squeezed through the conversation and tobacco smoke in the corridor, and out into the almost equal chatter and smoke in the Östergade. Then the godly stillness of the sleeping *pension*, the mute reproach of the lonely bedroom candle.

Our last day in Denmark sprang upon us as from an ambush, after the manner of last days, that are expected and feared, yet forgotten. The establishment, termed in the French of its proprietress "*Le Penksione,*" was busy with prophecies of evil; the lady with the green fringe enlivened the breakfast-table with news of the increase of cholera in Hamburg; the elderly Dane shook her head over the weather, and had a memory stored with depressing anecdotes of the crossing from Korsoer to Kiel. It could scarcely have been worse than the crossing to the Hôtel d'Angleterre on that gusty and dripping 5th of October. The man at the newspaper-stall inside the great hotel doorway, from whom we had been wont to buy an English paper, had none for us. Winter had fallen upon Denmark, and not before the following May would the voice of the *Standard* be heard in the land. We turned away, and drove in depression to the Houses of Parliament.

The Danish Rigsdag is unobtrusively located in a

OUR LAST DAY IN DENMARK

minor palace, up a side street; it looked like the sort of place one would go to about income-tax, such was the modest reserve of its entrance and swing doors, such the severe rectitude of its staircase. The friend who had so often sacrificed herself for our entertainment in Copenhagen met us at the doorway, and with little prelude of lobby or corridor

we were in the precincts of the Folkething, the Lower
House, a very large, low hall, with pillars and a great
deal of white and gold about it. The general suggestion was of the saloon of an ocean liner. The
benches of the legislators curved in horseshoe shape
to the rostrum of the Speaker; in front of each
member was a desk, set forth with writing materials
and Parliamentary returns, and in generous proportion to the number of members were duly ranged the
spittoons. The Prime Minister, Herr Estrup, was
speaking—a middle-aged senator of the English squire
type, with reddish-grey moustache and whiskers,
and something cat-like about his broad cheek-bones
and light, steady eye. It was a speech on the Budget,
spoken in a poor voice, and without any graces of
delivery. Little attention was paid to him; the
members talked, wrote letters, went out, or chatted
in whispers with the occupants of the space set apart
for visitors.

Incredible as it may seem to the British legislator,
we ourselves, with others of our dangerous sex, were
among the occupants of that space, and though the
sole barrier was a low, padded balustrade, we understand that it has hitherto served its purpose and
stemmed the invasion of the Women Suffragists.
The Eastern precautions that hedge our Ladies'
Gallery—whether in the interests of its occupants,
or of those of the Members, we have never clearly
understood—were here daringly neglected. It does
but show how quickly the mind becomes habituated
to abuses that it seemed quite unremarkable to see
a young woman walking upon the sacred floor of the
House itself, without a hat, without so much as a
veil, and with an unblushingly business-like aspect.
She was one of the reporters, and she moved about
and made her notes with apparent unconsciousness

of her singular privileges, while Estrup's low, monotonous voice continued its disquisition on the Budget.
Wearying as the speech appeared to be to its audience, it was one of an historical series, the last, in
fact, of that strange epoch during which a Minister,
supported by the King and the Upper House, held
his own against a majority of the Lower House.
Year after year the Folkething threw out his Budget,
year after year the Landsthing accepted it; but the
Landsthing having no power by itself, it became
necessary to collect the taxes by Royal decree, instead
of by Parliamentary order. It was absurd; in the
eyes of the Socialists it was blasphemy, but, like the
curse of the Cardinal in the " Jackdaw of Rheims "—

> " What gave rise to no small surprise,
> Nobody seemed one penny the worse ! "

The country throve in its quiet way, while the
Royalties grew yearly deeper into the popular affection, till, for the sake of national self-respect, the
Radicals last year compromised with a good grace;
and having passed his final Budget, Herr Estrup
retired victorious from the long contest, in the afterglow of the enthusiasm that flared round the silver
wedding of the Crown Prince.

We left him talking on among his sheaves of
statistics, and went upstairs to the Landsthing,
where everything was still more white and gold and
pillared than in the Folkething, and even more conspicuously like a steamer saloon. Here also the
lady reporter sat, and garnered at ease the murmurs
of a debate whose languid purport we have forgotten.
The members of the Landsthing are elected by voters
who must possess at least £130 a year; it may have
been trivial, but it was inevitable to note their
superiority in manner, in looks, in dress to the Lower

Chamber, where the members are elected by any or every Dane who is over twenty-five years of age, and has not the misfortune to be a felon, a bankrupt, a domestic servant, a lunatic, or a woman.

Calm and saloon-like are the memories of the Danish Parliament; its mild ornateness, its members meditating compromise and habitually drinking weak tea, its placid acceptance of uncaged womankind, its Minister approaching crisis and victory with the same *sang-froid* with which he had for nineteen years ignored defeat. And there calmness dies, slaughtered that evening by the urgent portmanteau, packed by slow torture to its final apoplexy, the dinner eaten in the expectancy of the cab and the paramount expectancy of seasickness.

Down the asphalte of the Östergade the *droitschke* went smoothly through the sauntering crowd; every one except ourselves at ease with the world, every one sipping the lamp-lit idleness of Copenhagen in infinite leisure. With a rattle over paving-stones, a wrench across tram-lines, we lurched away out of holiday; the true pang of parting was there, edged by fore-knowledge of long fatigues, of warfare with *douaniers,* of the certainty of missing the Hamburg train at Kiel. The central station seethed to the doors with a mob of tourists on their way home from Norway; there were but two seats left in the train, and they were in the hot heart of a crowded carriage; the netting was already full of small luggage, therefore ours must travel on our laps.

There was indeed a corner seat, but we could not but yield it to the English youth who was leaning out of the open window and saying good-bye to a Danish girl. He wore, according to Danish custom, the ring that betokens betrothal; her hand was in his, and they seemed to find conversation a difficulty.

The bell rang, the whistle sounded. He leaned still further from the window, and she lifted a face trembling with farewell.

We looked away.

MARTIN ROSS AND E. Œ. S.

September 1895.

THE ANGLO-IRISH LANGUAGE

(A consideration of Dr. P. W. Joyce's book
" English as we Speak it in Ireland ")

I⊤ would be as easy to coax the stars out of the sky
into your hat as to catch the heart of a language and
put it in a phrase-book. Ireland has two languages;
one of them is her own by birthright; the second of
them is believed to be English, which is a fallacy:
it is a fabric built by Irish architects with English
bricks, quite unlike anything of English construction. The Anglo-Irish dialect is a passably good
name for it, even though it implies an unseemly
equality between artist and material, but it is something more than a dialect, more than an affair of
pidgin English, bad spelling, provincialisms, and
preposterous grammar; it is a tongue, pliant and
subtle, expressing with every breath the mind of its
makers. When at its richest, in the mouths of the
older peasants, it owes most to Shakespearean England
—not in amount, but in quality. These old, quiet
people, fading now from us like twilight, with their
hearts full of undisturbed impressions, and their
memories clear and warm like mellowed engravings,
still use some of the English that came to Ireland
with Spenser, with Raleigh, with the Cromwellians,
the men who spoke the speech of John Bunyan, who
came, as Macaulay has said, with the praises of God
in their mouths and a two-edged sword in their
hands.

In the centuries that followed the Restoration the " Plantations " and the " Settlements " from England ceased, and Ireland slowly assimilated all. Gentlemen and peasants began to speak the same language, borrowing one from the other; the talk of the men of quality, bred in the classic tradition, enriched the vocabulary of the peasants, while the country gentlemen, themselves Irish speakers, absorbed into their English speech something of the vigour and passion, the profuse imagery and wilful exaggeration that are inherent in the Gael. Nowadays the talk that comes into Ireland from England, with its commercial slang, its facetious under-statement, its Cockney assurance, cannot be said to enrich the Anglo-Irish vocabulary; yet more direful are the contributions from America. To-day that nauseating term, " the Boss," is glibly used by the country people of the West; deep among the hills of Connaught, girls who have earned their dowries in New York factories and Philadelphia hotels, guess and calculate, and drawl and mew through their noses, to their own high satisfaction and to the respectful admiration of their relatives. Yet Anglo-Irish remains to us, a medium for poets and story-tellers that is scarcely to be surpassed, a treasury of idiom and simile meet for the service of literature.

But the spirit of the language is guarded by many dragons. Writers of various degree have tried a fall with them and have retired worsted, to construct from their inner consciousness the vision that was denied to them, even as the scientist constructed the camel. Shakespeare yielded once, and but momentarily, to the temptation; and it is impossible to say that he came out of it well. Even in his day there was a convention for an Irishman; and recognising it as such, he abandoned Captain Macmorris with all decent speed. But the convention lived on, and developed into that over-blown blossom of English humour, the stage Irishman. Thackeray knew something of the matter, yet Captain Macmorris and Captain Costigan are brothers in more than arms; Mr. Kipling understands much, but Private Mulvaney is of their company. They may bluster, weep, rollick, and make love; like " Mr. Dooley " of Chicago, their argument may be excellent, the interest of their stories indisputable; it is of no avail, their speech bewrayeth them, they are of the far-flung family of the Stage Irish. But, as a very young English curate said, addressing a large London congregation, " Dear people, we must not be too hard on the Apostles ! "

In the last five-and-twenty years Irish writers have begun to realise that the waters of Jordan at their feet are more potent, even more fashionable, than those of Abana and Pharpar; so fully aware, indeed, are they of their racial privileges that they have already succeeded in making Ireland self-conscious. She now insists on being taken seriously, and will no more pose as the Agreeable Rattle. Her precious gifts of humour and of laughter are in danger of extinction, gloomed over monotonously as they are by clouds laden with artistic tears. Ireland is to be treated as an invalid, and must be approached with the hushed step of the sick-room. We maintain that Ireland is not, and never can be, monotonous; she varies as inveterately as the flicker of shadow and sunlight in the leaves of spring; and literature that shuts out the sunlight is incomplete. Lady Gregory, and a few others in whom is the root of the matter, have understood how to use both, and know how to weave together the gold and grey. There was a countrywoman, quite innocent of literary tendencies, who got tidings that her son was ill in hospital. " Oh, God ! " she said, " there was a wing in my heart till I came to him." And having said this, having breathed this sigh of pure and perfect poetry, she went on to express her gratitude to the doctor. " Why then, the world knows he *is* a good docthor, and a great help to the Lord Almighty, though, faith ! "—and here she laughed—" sometimes it'd fail the pair o' thim ! " This woman had " the two ways in her, and a touch of the cross-roads," to use an ancient phrase of Anglo-Irish. Cross-roads were in the older times places where on Sunday afternoons the people met and danced and talked—places where the knavish speech did not sleep in the foolish ear.

Dr. P. W. Joyce's little book might well for second title have been called " Heard at the Cross-Roads." He has listened well, and listened in the right places, and records what he has heard with the ease of a scholar and the sympathy of a son of the soil. That his book is a small one is almost its only fault; on such a subject completeness is practically impossible. For beyond vocabulary and phrase, idiom and proverb, lie construction, the shape in which thought is born, the point of the mental attack, the moment in the metre of the sentence where the weight must fall. These can scarcely be set down, yet they govern all. It may safely be said that few sentences of any sustained length or intention are cast identically in English and Anglo-Irish. Dr. Joyce knows this, and knowing it, does not attempt the impossible; he is content to give us, loosely, the gleanings of a long life devoted to the study of Ireland, and gives them with a simple geniality and agreeability that turn what might have been an arid catalogue into an entirely entertaining and sociable volume. Three gifts must be pre-eminently his, and they are not freely bestowed on studious men—the happy knack of making others talk, the power of appreciation, and the selective memory. Casually, during many years, the examples have been jotted down; casually, among them, drop the illuminating comments; he does not hurry, he is never bored, and the jovial anecdote, the personal reminiscence, crop up everywhere. His harvest is reaped, as is but natural, among the peasants and the poor people of the towns; each upward step in the social scale is a step further from the Irish language and its enormous influences. Here and there he touches, but not perhaps with so certain a hand, the delicate task of differentiating between the formulas, shibboleths and phrases of the upper social grades. We respectfully differ from him when he states that " I am after finishing my work " —" I am after my dinner "—are expressions " universal in Ireland among the higher and educated classes "; or that " Sure I did that an hour ago," " Sure you won't forget," are " heard perpetually among gentle and simple." "I bought an umbrella the way I wouldn't get wet," and " I'd 'no is John come home yet," are also expressions with a grade of their own, and cannot be classed, as they are by Dr. Joyce, as " often used by educated people." Some exacter term is needed here. Education can belong to all grades, and education is only a rudiment of culture. It is old-established culture and social usage that decide upon these matters; and, for one reason or another, certain expressions have ceased to be current among the upper classes, while they remain suspended in the next grade or two. It was just here that Thackeray, in his desire for local colour, went wrong. Lever, working with a full and slovenly brush, washed in his local colour without an effort. He made his heroes talk like gentlemen; it was not necessary for him to rely upon provincialisms to show that they were Irishmen too. In the speech of the upper-class man or woman what is crudely called the " Irish brogue " is rarely present in its strength, yet their talk is full of the vivid quality that is theirs, partly by heritage, partly by intimacy with the people who were till almost yesterday their tenants. Sooner or later the skilled ear will recognise something in the intonation, in the careless extravagance of simile, in the instinct for effect and the wish to create it, that will betray that composite being, the Anglo-Irishman.

" So far as our dialectical expressions are vulgar or unintelligible," says Dr. Joyce, " those who are educated among us ought to avoid them." But the point we wish to make is that the Captain Costigan of real life would not have avoided them; it simply would not have occurred to him to employ them. This, from some points of view, is undoubtedly regrettable. Phrases such as those offered by Dr. Joyce—and let us here offer him our heartfelt thanks for his artistic reticence in the spelling of them—are worthy to sparkle on the stretched forefinger of all time; they add the pictorial quality to conversation, they give a tingling freshness to the common things of life. " He could quench a candle at the other side of the kitchen with a curse "; " He has forty-five ways of getting into his coat "; " The life of an old hat is to cock it "; " He's neither glad nor sorry, like a dog at his father's wake "; " A man looking at a carriage in motion says : ' Aren't the little wheels dam good not to let the big wheels overtake them ! ' " These, and throngs of others of their kind, mark the intolerance of the unvarnished fact and the brimming imagination that can and will embellish it. Proverbs and set phrases are ready in plenty, yet they do not satisfy the ambition of the artist. The variety of well-established blessings is enormous, yet in our own hearing a beggar woman, addressing a young soldier, has improvised this one : " My welcome home to ye in grandeur and in splendour ! Here's my dirty hand to ye, my lovely Captain ! That no angry ball may ever catch ye ! " In the same category of benediction may be recorded a Meath blessing that has escaped Dr. Joyce's net : " May you live so long that a spider would draw you to the grave." And again, as a coffin was entering a churchyard, a kneeling woman, shrouded in the long, dark cloak of Southern Munster, cried : " That your journey may thrive with ye ! "

Which brings us to a point noticeable in a collection so comprehensive and so sympathetic as Dr. Joyce's. The poetic phrase, that in Ireland " blooms and withers on the hill like any hill flower," and in a like profusion, is but sparsely represented in his book. A few, indeed, there are, and their quality is of the best : " You'd lead him there with a halter of snow "—this of a person secretly very willing to go to a place, as a lover to the house of the girl's parents ; " The breath is only just in and out of him, and the grass doesn't know of him walking over it." Of an unlucky man it is said : " He is always in the field when luck is on the road "—a picture drawn from the life of a people whose days are spent under the sky in the open country. " The road flew under him," is yet another, and, save these, we have discovered none that appeal to the sense of beauty.

One other trifling charge must be made. Into this collection there have crept many expressions neither native to Ireland nor specially interesting. It will certainly be news to most people that " Out of sight, out of mind," " Adam's ale," " Down in the mouth," " The other day," " A chip of the old block," " As many lives as a cat," and others of similar familiarity, are phrases that " belong to Ireland, though possibly

" CHILD O' GRACE ! IT'S NOT FOR THE SAKE OF A PINNY YOU AND ME'D
FALL OUT ! "

current in England or Scotland "; and we would submit that whatever dialectical interest they may once have possessed has been effaced by much handling. We could wish their places filled by more of Dr. Joyce's flashlights upon the Ireland of his youth. When he says, " In my boyhood days I knew a great, large, sinewy, active woman who lived up in the mountain gap, and was universally known as Thunder the Colt from Poulaflaikeen," we long for further details. If we venture to disagree with Dr. Joyce in his assertion that " Colt is often pronounced Cowlt," we do so in the spirit of the Munster beggar-woman who delicately rebuked a defaulting benefactor in the words, " Child of grace! It's not for the sake of a pinny you and me'd fall out ! "

E. Œ. S. AND MARTIN ROSS.

1910.

AN INCORRIGIBLE UNIONIST

THE Bog of Allen slid past the window of the railway carriage, in long floors of grey and brown, rifted with mauve; the horizon was level as a bowstring, and the grey sky arched to it. The unrest of Dublin fell back into its place among lesser things; the pageant of the Horse Show, the almost audible rustle of cheque-book and bank-note, the strikers standing ominously in Sackville Street with the Mounted Police watching them—all these were left behind like the heat of the day, and the mood of the sovereign countryside enforced itself. Like a sovereign it sent forth its representative, and he, the Horse, has with inimitable grace and distinction played his part before the nations, and added yet another touch of the paramount and the inexplicable to the reputation of Ireland. It is his prerogative to preserve and present, without incongruity or effort, the age of chivalry, to move, year after year, through the changeful crowd in the Dublin street as though he carried a Knight of the Round Table, to pass in through the soulless monotony of motors to his palace at Ball's Bridge, wild-eyed and splendid, or soft-eyed and wise, as he passed into the lists of Ashby-de-la-Zouch. Even as he stands, sheeted and dignified, in his place in the long streets of stalls, the turn of his polished quarters tells of his high lineage, of his power and his elegance; down to the clean straw his legs are unquestionably a gentleman's, longer, perhaps, than the English eye is accustomed to, but that is Ireland, and we like it so. There are more specimens of him this year than ever before, and more people to look at him, five or six thousand more people, but that is nothing to him; he has been looked at hard from the hour of his birth, and his virtues have been proclaimed before his shy face; he has evoked simile and epigram even while yet he hid behind his mother. He has also heard his detractors; they may even have accused him very loudly of " having no more bone than a dog," or of a habit of " boxing himself," or of having " a fashion of twining the leg," even of " going light on the former leg " (which, it may be explained, means being slightly lame in a fore), a matter at once met by the extenuating circumstance that he was " growing a splinter." Intense and untiring observation has been accorded to him throughout his life, therefore he moves in stately docility in the big rings, where the people lean thick to follow his movements, and the dealer beckons him to the rails, and the heated tide of encomium is met by the glacier stream of detraction, and out of these is brought forth, like a *chaud-froid*, the Bargain. He is passed on, probably, almost certainly, to England and to Germany, but that early life of his, among a clever people who expected him to be as clever and intuitive as they, has made him what he is, as surely as Galway limestone or Munster pastures have entered into his bones. Has not an English cavalry sergeant-major told the present writer, while looking on at " stables " at Aldershot, that the Irish horses who passed into the regiment learned their work in a noticeably shorter time than any other? So it should be with those of their upbringing.

It is, of course, in that unique jumping enclosure of Ball's Bridge, when he springs to his work, ignoring, in spite of his sensitive soul, the slope of faces in the enormous stand, the solid ring of them framing the long oval of grass, that he displays his greatest qualities. There, with every eye fastened on him, he rejoices as a giant to run his course, bold, resource-ful, and fulfilled with that enthusiasm that he squanders so lavishly in the chase. That intellectual countenance of his is set towards his old friends, the bank and the stone wall, taking their measure with practised eyes and pricked ears, as he comes at them over the dainty grass; he seizes the tall bank, poises on it like an acrobat, and as he kicks it from him is already making up his mind about the stone wall that follows on it. Over the stones he enjoys himself with less reserve than is demanded by that excellent piece of brainwork, the negotiation of the bank, but he does not forget the final upward fling of the hind legs to avoid the dislodging of a stone. Bank, water-jump, and hurdle follow, but water-jump and hurdle are tame after bank and wall, and do not exhibit the higher qualities of the artist in horse or rider. When a horse, in his eagerness, took off too soon and pecked heavily upon the bank, his rider most justifiably lost his stirrups, and every face followed the problem of whether or not he would recover them before the wall was reached. The pulling horse fought for his head, and spread himself mightily over the stones; the rider, stirrupless but unshaken, lay back to the big lift, and a " Ha ! " of skilled approval broke hard and simultaneous from the oval frame of spectators. It was somewhere here, while the pairs of competitors charged their fences, and the horses waiting for their turn danced like thistledown in the background, that lines by one of our own poets drifted back to me—

> " So bold and frank his bearing, boy,
> Did you meet him onward faring, boy,
> In Lapland's snow or Chili's glow,
> You'd say, ' What news from Erin, boy ? ' "

Over here we scarcely know what the news is, or will be. During this week people have asked each other, at Leopardstown, at the Show, at the Bloodstock Sales, at Phœnix Park Races, how things will be next year, when the Royal Dublin Society opens the doors of its forty-sixth Horse Show, and there has been no satisfactory answer. That incorrigible Unionist, the Horse, alone remains where he was, and will remain, like charity, the bond of peace. The army of foals now in the fields are pushing on towards their vocations; the men or women who watch over each have their hearts in his future, and that future is pure of politics. The world wants him more than ever now; Ulster and the South are producing him with an equal intentness in response to the great desire of other countries for him; Ireland herself will want him when the latest horse-drawn farming machinery is placed by co-operation within the reach of small farmers as well as large. He is knitting Ireland together; the political situation, heavy and black as it is, opens to let him through. When the wondrously blended crowd moves in the enclosured area of the Horse Show, and the seldom seen Union Jack lounges there on its staff, and the National Anthem makes there its resounding statement of faith, the Horse might laugh in his heart at his power to place such matters in a secondary position. But, unlike the dog, the Horse seldom laughs.

MARTIN ROSS.

September 1913.

IRELAND, THEN AND NOW

" JONAH," said an eminent authority to an ignorant disciple, into whose hands the *Recollections of Sir Jonah Barrington* had, for the first time, fallen, " Jonah is an interesting old liar." Which was at once stimulating and discouraging. The disciple, however, discouraged not much, remembering that the admixture of a lie doth ever add pleasure, addressed itself—the third person singular and neuter is here, in humility, substituted for the authoritative plural—to the small and pleasing green volume, and found the interest indisputable, while the lies, as is but usual with well-handled lies, did not, so far as the disciple (whose ignorance has been postulated) was aware, emerge. The writer of the lucid and interesting preface to the volume in question, says, " It is Sir Jonah Barrington who gives us the first fairly complete and authentic portrait of the rollicking Irishman of later literary tradition. . . . We get the tone, the colour of the men about whom he writes. We gain, as we read him, queer glimpses of an extraordinary society. We need not suppose that Barrington exaggerated the bacchanalian recklessness of the men who described themselves thus—

> " Beauing, belling, dancing, drinking,
> Breaking windows, damning, sinking,
> Ever raking, never thinking
>   Live the Rakes of Mallow."

We do not suppose it for an instant, even though the writer " declines to pin his faith to the accuracy of the details " given by Barrington of the " Match of Hard Going," described in Chapter V, as the method taken by a party of young foxhunters to dissipate the *ennui* of a period of frost. Shut up in the huntsman's cottage, with a hogshead of claret and a dead cow; provided by the family piper with " music's discourse most eloquent," seven young gentlemen, of birth and breeding, spent seven days and seven nights in devouring the cow, with the assiduity of a pack of hyænas, laughing hyænas, no doubt—Sir Jonah speaks affectionately of their " jollity and good humour "—but hyænas whose only indisputable claim to humanity can be based on their having emptied the hogshead of claret.

The preface may, in charity, refuse acceptance of these facts, yet it was the age of monstrous eating, of immoderate drinking. Not in Ireland alone did gentlemen, as our preface says, " drink, swagger, and behave like swine," nor did the singular theory obtain only in the eighteenth century, that the merits of " a good fellow " were decided by his capacity to assume the duties of a wine-barrel. There was a wine club among the undergraduates of a fashionable college at Oxford, what time the nineteenth century was young, that apportioned merit to its members in accordance with the number of corks of bottles of port that they could produce in evidence of their achievements during a sitting. And one of these members, as a grandfather, and a singularly abstemious grandfather, has acknowledged to a tally of six. Indisputably the Ireland of the self-satisfied twentieth century can furnish some incidents that might challenge comparison with Barrington's most purple patches; paler, perhaps, a little, but nevertheless of good fast colours. A tale is told, on sufficient authority, of a civic feast in an Irish provincial town, of which the details might have been gathered from the cheerful pages of Sir Jonah. Among its minor features is included a jig, danced on the dinner-table among wine-glasses, fruit, and flowers, but the incident that can claim most direct descent from Barrington's time was the fox-hunt that followed the feast. The name—let us say—of O'Shaughnessy, was one shared in that city by men of all degrees. Two of its most splendid exponents held, at the close of the dinner, converse together, and while, splendidly, erect upon the hearth-rug, they discoursed of the dinner, the weather, and Home Rule, a third O'Shaughnessy, very small and abject, but temporarily glorious with unusual champagne, advanced upon them. Encircling, as far as he could, the white waistcoats of his namesakes with a sudden embrace, he cried in a passion of tribal pride, " Here we are ! Three O'Shaughnessies ! And in the Globe of Ireland there doesn't stand our aiquals ! "

With this he was immediately struck to the ground by his clansmen, and before he could rise to his feet, a playful gentleman in a pink evening coat uttered the scream that is usually dedicated to the last moments of a fox, and flung himself, as it were a hound, upon the repudiated one. Freeing himself by force of panic-frenzy from his attacker, the humble O'Shaughnessy took to his heels, the City Fathers, headed by the gentleman in the hunt-coat, following, with such cries as conformed best with their various ideals of the sounds proper to the hunting-field. The pursuit burst from the banqueting-chamber, and went at large through the surrounding passages. The quarry may, or may not, have been " broken up " according to the rules of the chase; the story, for our purpose, ends here. But it may be conceded that the Ireland of Barrington and Lever has still its standard-bearers.

In some ways, however, it is the points of divergence between the Ireland of Then and Now that are the more salient. In the chapter entitled " Patricians and Plebeians," Barrington unhesitatingly divides Irish country society into four classes; these are the Common People, Half-mounted Gentlemen, Gentlemen every inch of them, and Gentlemen to the backbone. The difference between the two latter orders was one of money only, and would seem to have been scarcely worthy of definition, but the barriers between the Gentlemen, the Peasants, and the " Half-mounted " (or, as a later use has it, " Half-sirs ") were practically unassailable. These barriers are shaking now; abolished, says the new school of patriots, eagerly anticipating that *écrasement* of the exclusive order of the " Gentlemen to the Back-bone," to which their most strenuous efforts are directed, unaware of their own at least equal exclusiveness, who deny to any save themselves the right to be called the people of Ireland. It is singular that the spread of education, even of such education as has been thought good enough for Ireland, and the influx of American ideas, should have evolved the very bigoted insularity which characterises that party which is certainly the noisiest, if it is not the most important, in the Ireland of 1918.

It is only those who do not know Ireland who offer pronouncements about her; yet it may be said that it is hard to believe that these immature Republicans represent that well-loved Ireland, that " dear Isle in the Waters," whose place is hidden deep in our hearts; harder still to believe that they are sincere in the faith they proclaim. Irishmen may, and often do, trumpet their conviction of their transcendent superiority, but it is the very heart of self-distrust that is in them that often inspires their vehemence.

The Irishman is an idealist, a worshipper of idols, of things higher than himself. Beyond all men he can adore a cause, a religion, a party; yes, and if he be of the order of " The Common People," the family under whose sway he has first known life. Miss Edgeworth and Barrington alike testify to the devotion that has so often in the past flamed into self-sacrifice for the beloved master, and that, even in the present, has still some seed of fire in it. But it was a flame that the " Half-mounted " had no power to light. The peasants of the eighteenth century were of the true order of idealists, and asked only that their God should be consistent and act as a God; he must stamp upon them rather than stoop to them.

The writer has memories of an old lady who, seeing her grandchild holding converse with a workman, a mower of grass, called imperiously from her window, bidding the mower to continue his mowing and the child to cease from talking. But the mower, who had grown grey in the service of the old lady, did but respect her the more.

But Sir Jonah's chapters on the Irish Gentry of his own and earlier times, and of their retainers, crush the spirit out of later recitals. The taking of Castle Reuben, with " Jug Ogie's " successful espionage, and Keeran Karry's battles on behalf of his mistress and her castle. The presentation of the ears of a disapproved-of acquaintance in response to an idle wish. " Sure, my lady," says old Ned Regan, the butler, " you wished that Dennis Bodkin's ears were cut off, and here they are; and I hope you are plazed, my lady ! " It must reluctantly be conceded that these are patches of a Tyrian purple that cannot now find their equals.

There are few things stranger, or more difficult to understand, than "the two ways "—according to an old saying—that are in every Irishman. How can the personal charm and gentleness, the tenderness with children, the consideration for women, be reconciled with the cruelties that have stained the early rebellions, the barbarities to animals that have

"IT ISN'T THE MAN I RESPECTS, BUT THE OFFICE"

degraded the later agrarian warfare? It has been said that the Irishman alone, and the Irishman of the crowd are different beings. Let us, perforce, leave it at that. But in another aspect "the two ways" are equally remarkable. We have spoken of the Irishman's blatant patriotism and of his secret self-distrust; it is of the operation of "the two ways" that the self-contempt can sometimes be so nakedly expressed as to afflict the hearer. We have heard an old Irishman characterise lying as "a dirty, low habit of the Irish"; a prosperous Irish farmer has declared that his greatest ambition in life was to be "mistaken" for an English gentleman—a double-edged mistake that the mere expression of such a wish puts beyond the bounds of possibility. This is not the race whose spirit will find expression in the Republic of Sinn Fein aspirations. A story is told of the Rising in Dublin in Easter week, 1916. An English visitor, deploring its results, spoke of it as a Rebellion. "Ah, that wasn't a rebellion at all!" said the Irishman—"that was no more than a row. Sure ye couldn't call that a rebellion. There was no gentry in it!"

Ireland exacts an object of adoration, even an abstraction; a Throne, though the king were unworthy; a Church, though the representative of Heaven cannot be revered. There was a priest in a remote country parish who was disliked by his flock, and, which is rarer, despised. A poor woman discussed him with a neighbour of the other faith. "Sir," she said, "it isn't the man I respects, but the office."

Miss Edgeworth, in her memoirs, quotes her father, who was a reformer and an enthusiast, as "contending" that there is "a fund of goodness in the Irish as well as in the English nature," an opinion which might now seem a truism, but was then regarded as a token of philanthropic eccentricity. "The misfortunes of Ireland," says Mr. Edgeworth, "were owing not to the heart, but to the head; the defect was not from nature, but from want of culture." Sir Jonah Barrington, on the other hand, like many of his class, accepted the Irish character with an amused pessimism, and dismisses the Irish peasant with " one sweeping observation, namely, that the brains and tongues of the Irish are somewhat differently formed or furnished than those of other people." The Irishman may be dismissed with an epigram, or a curse, but, as England knows, he has a way of recurring. Even Barrington, with all his pessimism, admits that " a good steady Irishman will do more in an hour, when fairly engaged upon a matter which he understands, than any other countryman." He spoke of the educated Irishman. " The lower orders," he is careful to add, " exhibit no claim to a participation in the praise I have given to their superiors." It would seem to a present-day observer that Edgeworth and Barrington, approaching the matter from opposite poles, met at the vital point, which is Education. Vital to-day as it was when Richard Edgeworth, in his daughter's words, "turned the attention of the House " (*i. e.* the Irish House of Commons) "to a subject which he considered to be of greater and more permanent importance than the Union, or than any merely political measure could prove to his country, the Education of the people."

A POOL OF SILOAM

It is 2 p.m. of a hot southern May day. My neighbour, the dotard, has gone to sleep. We are seated, he and I, on either side of a machine resembling a fossil tortoise, erect on its tail, rampant. Flexible tubes connect us with the machine, tubes that also connect horribly with the warm and windy interior of the tortoise. A sulphurous gale pants down my throat in varying temperatures, now bleakly dry, now sultry damp. My neighbour's tube, aimed at the prominent second button of his waistcoat, vents itself, innocuous for good or evil. The *baigneur*, a broad, hot man in shirt sleeves, has discovered him, has hustled him back to a sense of his position. He laughs guiltily at me, conscientiously absorbing the breath of the tortoise.

It is a huge vaulted room, with a similar apparatus in each corner. Open-mouthed greybeards surround each, looking like starving elderly fledgelings. They croak hoarsely to each other of their ailments. I am regarded as beyond the pale, and receive neither sympathy nor confidence. I close my eyes and the warm varying gusts play vagrantly over my face. I fancy I am on the top of a Paris tram with the roar of traffic and the prattling of French in my ears. The sky is very blue; there is a smell—yes, decidedly they have been asphalting the——

" *Ne faut pas dormir !* " says a voice. I see by the arch expression of the dotard that he considers himself avenged.

Outside, along the white limestone steps, in chairs

and on benches, sit in parboiled rows the victims of their systems, and of that of the Établissement Thermal d'Aix-les-Bains. They suggest a wearied congregation who have collapsed at the doors of the church. Above them towers the huge white façade, with its three high-arched portals, and its wide, high flights of steps. For this Pool of Siloam is set half-way up a steep hill, and one mounts rather than descends to its healing waters. Echoing stone galleries extend right and left from the domed central hall, where a little twelve-year-old Egeria sits by the first visible manifestation of the Source, dealing tepid tooth-glassfuls from the three taps of alum, sulphur and plain cold water, under her control. Egeria sometimes nods; with the music born of hurrying water ever in her ears and breakfast at 4 a.m. it can scarcely be wondered at. For at 5 a.m. the Établissment opens its wide doors, and the staff, from the magnificent gold-laced, scarlet-bosomed concierge, down to little Egeria, are in waiting till eleven, and again from two till five p.m.

In all the various " Cercles," and Purgatory can scarce boast more, the mermen and merwomen are scouring and kneading impotent items of humanity, whose proportions, as viewed at *table d'hôte*, suggest now a feather bed, now a sketching easel. Personally, in a matter of massage, I should prefer to practise on a sketching easel. Sleepy men in shabby uniform line the long corridors. Beside them stand the *chaises-à-porteurs*, sedan chairs, hybrid between a hearse and a puppet-show. The patients, swathed in blankets, are borne home in these mute, mysterious conveyances. The bath attendant supplies the name of the hotel and the number of the room—it is on record that embarrassing mistakes have not seldom been made—and then all is silence. Sometimes a hooded face may peer, like Lazarus in his grave-clothes, between the striped curtains; sometimes below the lower drapings, objects like the feet of a white elephant may show, but for the most part there is nothing to tell the bystander that a fellow-creature is near; nothing, save the beads of perspiration on the porters' brows, the eloquent droop of their well-laden shoulders.

.   .   .   .   .

I sit in one of the two dressing-rooms appropriated to each *Cabinet des Bains.* Without, down the long cloistral corridors—it is, to be precise, the *Galeries des Princes Neufs* — I hear the shuffling of heavy feet as the red and white catafalques go by. From the inner seclusions come strange sounds—gasps and gurglings, shrill cries of encouragement and well-simu-lated enjoyment—and through all and over all, the ceaseless rushing of many waters.

" C'EST BON ! 'EIN ? "

" *C'est bon !* *'Ein ?* " says a hoarse, gay little voice, the voice of Benoite, head-inquisitress.

" *Oui, c'est bon,*" is responded in somewhat de-plorable English accents.

" *Et v'la une bonne tasse de café !* " says the vivacious Benoite.

I know that this is the formula in tendering a cup of warm sulphur water. The victim makes no audible reply, and the sluicing begins again. Then the ever-gleeful *baigneuse*—

" *Houp-lá !* *Lá, et lá !* " and the twin door of the dressing-room slams, and Benoite opens my

cell and greets her twelfth victim with unabated
cheerfulness.

She has been at work since 5 a.m. scouring and
slapping four patients per hour, and she will continue till eleven, but neither her spirits nor her
muscles flag. These are a race to themselves, these
little sturdy *baigneuses*. From the time when the
Romans built the great pale arch that faces the
Établissement, and downwards, their ancestresses
have been *masseuses*, and they have paddled through
all the generations in the healing streams of La
Source. One who saw them at 11 a.m. in their
plain black gowns, trooping down the wide steps,
and, as it happened, joining in the ranks of a troop
of similarly black-robed priests, said that the solu-
tion of their existence was then given to him. A
superannuated priest became a *baigneuse*—or perhaps *vice versa*—less plausible theories have proved
correct.

My last memory of Aix comes to me with a waft
of burning air, and of the scent of incense and rose-
leaves. A long, long procession, of priests, and choir-
boys, and nuns, and little cropped-headed children
dressed as angels, and more children, and yet more,
from all the schools of Aix, trails past the long,
shallow steps of the Établissement that are thronged
with curious *Étrangers* and more or less devout
natives. A rose-decked altar, in honour of the
" *Fête Dieu*," has been erected in one of the arched
entrances of the baths; a brief mass is sung, and
then this survival of mediæval, possibly Pagan rites,
winds, chanting, between the trees and the flower-
stalls and the china booths, into the ancient church,
and the show is over. As far at least as *M. M. les
Étrangers* are concerned. These, looking at their
watches, recognise gladly that the serious appetite

induced by the baths has not much longer to be endured. Through the solemn clanging of the church bells they hear the shriller summons of their various hotels, the inspiring clamour that tells of *déjeuner*.

P

A FOXHUNT IN THE SOUTHERN HILLS

THAT the seventeenth day of March should be established as the birthday of Ireland's chief Saint is of the nature of a compromise.

There is an old song, with an old tune, artless as it is consciously roguish, that expounds the position—

> " On the eighth day of March
>   (Or so some people say)
> Saint Patrick at midnight,
>   He first saw the day.
> But others declare
>   'Twas the ninth he was born,
> So 'twas all a mistake
>   Betwixt midnight and morn ! "

The song, however, goes on to say that Father Mulcahy (" who showed them their sins ") having assured his flock that " no one could have two birthdays, barrin' a twins," suggested that they should not be " always dividin'," but should " sometimes combine. Combine eight with nine, sivinteen is the mark—

> " 'Let that be his birthday !
> Amin ! says the clerk.' "

In spite, however, of Father Mulcahy's ingenious compromise, the celebrants of St. Patrick's Day have not often failed to find an excuse for breaking a head or two in his honour. Head-breaking reasons are still as plenty as ever in Ireland, and " risings " are prophesied as confidently by political prophets as are " depressions from the S.W. with wind and much

210

"LITTLE LAKES AND STRETCHES OF TAWNY BOG FILL ALL THE LEVEL PLACES"

rain " by those who allot to us our daily share of the weather.

Nevertheless, one speaks of the ford as one finds it, and there still remain far-away places of Southern Ireland where tranquillity broods, and friendliness to all and sundry, and, above all, friendliness to foxhunters and foxhounds, is firm and flourishing.

Yet it may confidently be asserted of one such place that a country less fitted by Providence for foxhunting would be far to find. A landscape must be pictured wherein little lakes and stretches of tawny bog fill all the level places, and, where these are not, the rest of the world is hillside, grey with rock, dark with furze and heather. Squeezed in among the rocks are the white cottages, with a crooked ash-tree, and a willow or two, between them and the south-west gales, each with its weedy patch of potatoes, and its enforced portion of tillage, drawn up about its knees like a brown blanket.

It was at a harsh and hideous National School (adjectives that are unhappily appropriate to most Irish National Schools) that the long hack, fifteen miles from Kennels, came to an end, and, as hounds and huntsman halted under its whitewashed walls, the war-time field, the few faithful women and farmers who had followed the Hunt into the wilderness, might have been justified in thinking that the " rising," so often foretold, had at length taken place.

Suddenly and incredibly the bare and quiet country became alive. Not a ridge of hill but had its black fringe of figures, hardly a fence but a lad or two was slipping over it as lithely as a fox. The boys of two parishes were afoot, and there was not a self-respecting young man among them but had " risen " to join the hunt.

It was a mild and beaming day, with spring fluting

in the larks' throats, and dancing in the wind that set the catkins on the willows tossing like little green lambs' tails. The furze-bushes were heaped with gold, and drenched with a scent as of apricots; the grass of the tiny pasture fields was green as the most translucent jade (which has a hue incomparably fairer and sweeter than an emerald can show). At the end of a long valley of bog the mountains were azure and mauve; the nearer hills went through wallflower tones of bronze and brown to orange, where the dead bracken held the sunlight, or palest topaz, in the sedge that spread upwards from the low ground into the ravines through which the streams ran down to the bogs. Along the wall of the schoolhouse yard went a dazzling frieze of children's faces; lovely faces, some of them, with the wonderful hair and eyes, and the glowing cheeks, that are bred of the soft breezes of these southern hills. Nothing save the clattering twitter of a flock of starlings could compare with the sound that ceaselessly proceeded from the frieze; only the children themselves could sever a syllable from that torrent of swift speech. The schoolmaster, a tall and portly person, with a moustache like the mane of a chestnut horse, was one of the leading sportsmen, and had indeed indited the mellifluous letter that had invited the Hunt to the hills. In scarcely less mellifluous terms he now explained the " most probable resort of the foxes," and having rounded his last period, he delivered the visitors into the hands of one whom he described as " a competent local Sisserone." The Sisserone, a black-bearded farmer, stout and middle-aged, yet of tireless activity, affably accepted the Hunt as a composite godchild, and took on sole responsibility with alacrity.

" We'll bate the bog below," he announced, " and if the game isn't there we'll make for the mountain ! "

It was an impressive programme. Either the bog or the mountain might have seemed a sufficiently serious proposition, but Mikey-Dan (which is neither Japanese nor Russian, and is merely the hyphenated title by which the middle-aged farmer was made known to his godchildren) had no shade of hesitation in his decisions. Without further preamble he lowered himself down a steep drop out of the road into a boggy field.

" Bring on the dogs ! " he ordered briefly.

" Huic over ! " said the huntsman, with an equal brevity, and the hounds flowed over the lip of the road, like water out of a basin, and followed Mikey-Dan.

So also did the few riders and the many runners. Born in the blood of the Irish country boy is the love of a horse. Hounds to him are no more than dogs, things of small account with which one turns cattle; mean creatures, to be treated meanly. But the horse, and especially the " hunting-horse," is a gentleman, and is revered as such. To see hounds run, they might say, is good, and it is a pleasant thing to behold the death of a fox, but what are these to watching a big-jumped horse throw a lep ! There once befell a blank day in the country now being treated of, and the master (who was riding a " big-jumped " mare) deplored to a farmer friend the disappointment that the lack of sport must have caused. He had forgotten the many and bizarre obstacles that had occurred during the day's fruitless wanderings. Not so the friend.

" Arrah, what disappointment had they ? No ! But they were well pleased. Kitty filled their eye ! "

The " bateing for game " involved a sufficiency of dramatic interest, even though the leading gentleman of the piece, " Charles James " himself, was not on in the first scene. The art of *camouflage* has been studied with remarkable success by the bogs of this district, and after one horse had gone down by the head, even to his ears, and another by the stern, so that nothing was left of him above ground but the makings of a hobby-horse, and this in spots that might have been selected as putting-greens, riders began to feel that to find a fox might impart a live-liness beyond what was desired. Presently there ensued a boundary-drain, deep and intimidating, that looked as if it had been dug out of wedding-cake and filled with treacle.

" Could we walk through it ? " suggested some one.

" You could not," replied Mikey-Dan, " that'd shwally the Kayser and all his min ! "

A war-time jest that was felt to be extremely smart and suitable for distinguished visitors.

The drain was not very wide, but it was wide enough, and what it economised in width it spent in depth. A place to gallop at, faintly trusting the larger hope that your horse will not refuse. But though the bog in which it is possible to gallop may exist in some favoured region, in Dereeny Bog it is not done—not, at least, by The Best People, who were undoubtedly those *intelligentzia* who unhesitatingly turned and hurried back, half a mile, to a bridge.

The hounds made no delay, and pitched themselves across, with backs hooped like shrimps, the remaining horses, trembling (like their riders) in every limb, were half-coaxed, half-goaded into following them. One only, a cob ridden by a girl, failed to make a good landing, and the speed and skill with which the attendant cloud of witnesses pulled the girl off his back, and caught his head, and successfully aided his efforts, was memorable.

It was not long after the drain episode that hounds

found. They had quickened their pace after the crossing, and that unmistakable throb of purpose had come into their researches which, after a blank draw, lifts the huntsman's heart. They spread themselves over the coarse sedge and rushes, and drew together with the eager sound that is more a whistle than a whimper, and then, just as hope was deepening to certainty, some watchers on the hill above the bog uttered those yells that, however habituated the hearer may be, have the quality that goes straight to the spinal marrow.

In an instant every-thing was running—hounds, country boys, a spancelled donkey, a pair of coupled goats; and the half-dozen riders, regardless of the practice of The Best People, were splashing and floundering across

A MUNSTER COUNTRY BOY

the bog after them. After the bog came a slope of rocks and furze, then a towering fence of stones and briars, unjumpable save at a "gap" (attractively filled with long, thin slabs of stone, laid across it like the knives of a mowing-machine). A short struggle up and across the "lazy-beds" of a patch of potato-ground, and then the panting horses heaved themselves up a cattle-passage that resembled the shaft of a lift, and on to the road. And when they got there the hounds and the country boys were gone as though they had never been.

A woman was knitting in the sun at a cottage door. She was a kind woman, and as the wild-eyed riders emerged, strenuously, from the lift, she arose and waved her knitting largely at the hill behind her little house.

"They're away up the mountain entirely!" she called to them.

The huntsman, with a face already redder than his coat, drove his horse in a turkey-cock rush across the road and over the bank.

The hillside rose sheerly above him. Little mellow flecks of sound came down, and told that the hounds also were above him. There are not many things more hateful than fighting up a hill that is so steep that a rapidly extending view of the horse's back-bone is presented to the rider, but when hounds are out of sight many hateful things can happen unheeded, and a great deal can be done in five minutes, and, in rather less than that time, the huntsman, and those few who clave to him, reached a level place—as it were a wider step in a stair-case—and made a pause. An appealing, questioning note on the horn was flung to the hilltop, and "a voice replied, far up the height," "Hurry on! They're this way!"

The mountain rose, in successive steps, sometimes heather and grass, more often bog, each step propped with a cliff of grey rock, and only to be gained by means of a connecting ravine.

The huntsman, after the manner of his kind, was slipping ahead; a despairing shout from one of his following caught him but just in time.

"Mike! if ye see them, for God's sake give a roar to us!"

Thus might Androcles have adjured his friendly lion.

A waft of hounds' voices, sweeter at that moment than the songs of Paradise, came down the wind to the little striving company.

" Oh, get on ! get on ! " says the girl on the cob, madly.

On the top of the mountain, a place that can best be likened to the carapace of a turtle, they caught the pack, checked for a moment, in the great wind that ever hurls over these high places. Mikey-Dan and a few of the elect were there also, watching with wary, narrowed eyes the opposite face of the nearest of the surrounding hills, whose rise and swell ceases only in that far-shining ocean which had suddenly leaped into view. The riders, arriving one by one, breathless, but happy again, received their praises proudly.

" Ye proved good ! ye did, faith ! And the horses too ! It's a tough chase, but they'll have him yet ! "

And with the words the hounds hit it once more, and were away over the shoulder of the hill through the heather, with a breast-high scent, and with a cry more tuneable than lark in any right-thinking shepherd's ear.

It was downhill this time, and the going was better. This side of the mountain had in some by-gone time been fenced, and a succession of stone walls of every type imparted an element of pleasing uncertainty. High single walls of lace-like open-work that toppled at a touch; wide banks of small stones on which the horses changed feet with a crashing rattle; upright spikes of rock with slanting spikes between, the interstices crammed with small stones; the southern Irish farmer plays tricks with his material with an infinite variation, and the southern Irish horses jump his achievements with an infinite zest. It is hard to define wherein lies the peculiar delight of a hunt in the hills. In description it is the difficulties that fill the picture, but in the happy rider's mind it is the glories that remain, the times when hounds are storming on the line, carrying a head like a flood in a river, and horses are pulling hard on the down-grade, and no man living can predict the fox's point.

This particular fox steered a good course, and, crossing a grassy valley, bore away into moorland again. The runners, hardy though they were, had long since been beaten. The last heard of them was a shout from Mikey-Dan.

" It's into the say he's running, he's that much afraid o' ye ! "

But Mikey-Dan was mistaken. In the middle of that desolate moor-country there stands a cliff that is like a tremendous door, closing an entrance to the heart of a hill. Old stories murmur about that mighty door, but what is behind it, a dead King, a Cluricaun's treasure, a Phuca, or a pathway to Fairyland, they do not dare to tell. The door is not a good fit; there is a space beneath it, hollowed out, one imagines, by the stream that flees from those hidden mysteries. The stories are afraid to tell us what they think is there, but in the minds of the hounds there was no uncertainty. They told us that the fox was there, and they said it at the tops of their voices, and made no secret about it.

THE CREW WHO SLOPPED AND SCRABBLED IN THEIR VARIOUS MEDIA OF
BLACK AND WHITE

"EN COSTUME DE VILLE"

" Montrez plusieurs poses, s'il vous plait ! "

The army of savages clustered round the stove run with hideous barefooted nimbleness to the model stand, and leap or scramble on to its dirty platform. Having gained that eminence they abandon themselves to nightmare realisations of the emotions. A Jewish youth, with eyes like a lizard, becomes an embodiment of Faith and Prayer. A little Italian, with a body of Dachshund-like proportions, swashbucklers it, a salvage man rampant, his stumpy legs wide apart, and a rusty file in his hairy fist. He is as hairy all over as a monkey, and his eyes roll in his motionless head as he tries to see how many hands go up in his favour.

" Trois ! Quat' ! Cinq ! Pas assez, descendez ! "

Two or three patriarchs, whose ancient persons are desolately in need of the watch-chains and double-breasted waistcoats proper to their age, rival one another in exemplifying Patience, Resignation, and other qualities supposed to befit the aged. There is a horribly plaintive anxiety in their eyes as they count the uplifted hands of the students, hands that hold a week of plenty, or of leanness in their grimy grasp. Their ribs utter eloquent appeals; they are so many bones of contention over which wrangle the artistic and the merely humane instincts; generally, it is to be feared, to the discomfiture of the latter. Scraggy Italian boys, suggestive in hue alike of the soot-bag and the lemon; haggard Frenchmen, with huge flat feet that have flattened and spread during long, patient hours of posing : all these, and more, in wearisome reiteration, until a sufficiency of hands has decreed the elevation of one of the gang to be for a week the exponent of the marvels of the human form.

There comes a time when the soul, however enthusiastic or industrious, turns in nausea from its expected task. Scarce, even, has the ardently-desired, if moderately-expressed, approval of the Professor, "*Presque pas mal,*" power to cheer or charm. Maybe it is the hint of spring in the air, a suggestion of the rioter who will so soon come rapping at the studio windows with fat, brown horse-chestnut buds, and will send the wheeling shadows of the swallows to give distracting hints of sunshine and irresponsibility. Perhaps the owner of the industrious and enthusiastic soul referred to ignores these things, and, bringing his attention back to the model —"*en clignant bien les yeux,*" as his Professor has so often ordained—finds that while he was absent in the spirit, the factious at the other side of the studio have radically altered the pose, and his drawing has leaped the narrow gulf that lies between mediocrity and absurdity. He knows it is useless to expostulate, he knows it is his own fault, he knows also that the Professor will arrive to correct in the course of the next five minutes.

The model causes ripples of shuddering to flow to and fro on his yellow body.

"*Le poele s'éteint !*" says some one, and it occurs to our friend that he is nearest the coal-box and must fulfil the unattractive office of stoker.

A ray of sun has sneaked round a stack of chimney-pots down through the great skylight of the studio; the dust dances in it. The shrill Alpine piping of the Auvergnois with the goats, sounds redolent of morning and brightness.

The Idle Apprentice stays not to stow his *carton*, but flees, as it were, in his naked feet from the responsibilities of the stove, and gets him swiftly out into the cheerful highways of the Quartier Latin. It may be that he has quieted his conscience with an undertaking to make quick sketches in the streets, or in the Luxembourg Gardens, an exercise often enjoined by the Professor. But no one who has not tried can know how futile and baffling such sketching can often be. The Argus-eyed "*Gardiens*" have first to be eluded, as, for some reason best known to the Parisian authorities, it is absolutely forbidden to sketch animate or inanimate nature in public gardens or galleries. Even if a sheltering bush affords a screen from their vigilance, the perambulating models, yea, even the models in perambulators, of which the Gardens yield so rich a crop, move or are moved as if by instinct from the concealed artist.

There remain the streets; a bench in the wide Boulevard St. Michel—the "*Boul' Miche*'," centre and epitome of the Quartier Latin—is a position that provides subjects of infinite variety and interest. But after a page or two has been filled in with flat-brimmed top hats and abundant *chevelures*, with indications of as much of the subsequent costume as an instant's glance has impressed on the retina, this also is apt to pall. It is a strange thing how inherent a reluctance the average human being feels to his or her commemoration on paper. This might, perhaps, be understood if the commemoration were exhibited, but, as a rule, before more than the hat of the model has been suggested, the artist eye has communicated its inevitable warning, and the maid whom he, as the poet says, has singled from the world, hurries out of range with every appearance of offence. Is this humility or is it spite? An opinion of human nature that has been embittered by many such reverses inclines me to the latter theory.

It was after a week or so of these out-of-door futilities, where every second person who passed along the pavements was " a subject," while not one of them could be satisfactorily garnered in the sketch-book, that it occurred to a few brave spirits that it might be possible to steer a middle course between the great heart of the nation in the streets and the unclad alien in the studios. These, by a happy inspiration, consulted a lady of high intelligence and authority, the *concierge* to whom they daily truckled and bowed down, Madame Rougemont.

" *Tiens !* " said Madame Rougemont, with several refined Parisian oaths, as she peered forth at her supplicants from the recesses of her dark and rankly-furnished den, " *ces Messieurs* demand models in the costume of every day? *Et vous payerez h'm, h'm, h'm——*"

In effect, the whole affair was to be left to her. One is not the *concierge* of a Quartier Latin rookery for nothing, and the acquaintanceship that such a position involves is both extended and peculiar. What delicate negotiations were undertaken by Madame Rougemont on behalf of those students will never transpire, but it is an undoubted fact that on the evening, and at the hour appointed by them, a model such as they had hitherto sought in vain presented himself at the tortuous, vine-draped passage that led to their studio in the Rue de la Grande Chaumière; a swarthy workman, in his sky-blue linen suit, whitened with plaster, and stained with work. He had brought his spade, his boots were still encrusted—O true Madame Rougemont !—with

the mortar of the afternoon's job. Moreover, forti-
fied during the pause by coffee and cognac, he posed
as though for a prolonged photograph. The stipu-
lated two hours sped by like a delirious dream. If
the model stood in need of restoratives, how much
more did not the artists require! By ten of the
inexorable clock these enthusiasts for the Realisation
of the Streets were aware that a couple of hours at
this high pressure were to the placid studio week as
fifty years of Europe to a cycle of Cathay, but they
wiped their warm brows and enjoyed it.

Thenceforth for some time the supply of models
equalled the demand. A *chiffonière*, the perfume of
whose basket left no doubt as to its genuineness;
a "*pauv' enfant de soldat*," son of one of Madame
Rougemont's most particular friends, who created a
sensation by fainting in the middle of the séance;
an ambiguous person, who, whether a "religious" or
no, had become possessed of a Brown Friar's habit
and looked the part; an old lady with one eye, who
sold dandelions, and performed a similar office to
the class by going away without warning at the end
of the first hour; all these took their turn to pose
in the dirty, picturesque atelier in the Rue de la
Grande Chaumière. It was a bi-weekly entertainment, and its promoters waxed proud as its fame
spread, and outsiders from other studios asked to
be allowed to join, and the crew who slopped and
scrabbled in their various media of black and white,
crowded thicker and thicker round the model "*en
costume de ville*." That was how Madame Rougemont described the attire of her clients.

There came, however, an evening when, at the
appointed hour, the model-stand was still vacant.
The promoters consulted together in darkling whispers; their irresponsible adherents jibed and mur-

Q

A CHIFFONIÈRE

mured in about equal proportions. The owner of
the studio, a conscientious but unpicturesque person,
proposed to immolate himself upon the altar of art.
The suggestion was received by his colleagues without
enthusiasm. The fortunes of the class visibly tot-
tered, when a tap was heard at the studio door.
Vainly endeavouring to conceal his ecstasy, the
studio's owner hastened to the door. He had expected the elderly milkman whose morning unpunc-
tuality was the theme of some of Madame Rougemont's
most impassioned invective. He had even arranged
a suitably abusive greeting, but a lady, young and
charming, met his gaze. He stood, stricken to
silence by astonishment, but the lady's self-possession
did not falter. She understood that Monsieur required a model, she mentioned her "*conditions*,"
and before Monsieur had more than realised what
bad French he spoke, she had crossed the room and
posed herself on the model stand. It is to his credit
that he induced his fellows to believe he had arranged
the whole affair.

The lady posed to perfection, read a novel in
decorous retirement near the stove during the ten
minutes' pause, and, at the end of the evening,
carefully counted the earnings that were placed
deferentially in her small, gloved hand, and was
again lost in the mystery of the night. Madame
Rougemont had no explanation to offer; the solitary
working hypothesis is that the sitting amounted
to an act of indemnity, consequent on financial
difficulties between the Lady and the Milkman.

'*NOT* THE WOMAN'S PLACE'

TIME was when there were but few forms of healthy, normal enjoyment to which these words, pregnant of prunes, prisms, and prisons, did not apply. Regarding the matter dispassionately, by the light of literature as well as that of social history, it would seem that the sole places on God's pleasant earth to which this warning placard was not affixed were those wherein The Woman was occupied with her dealings with the other sex; directly, as in the ballroom, or indirectly, as in the nursery. The indoor traditions of the harem governed the diversions and relaxations of the early Victorian ladies. The few exceptions proved—to quote for the thousandth time the age-worn aphorism—a rule that did not indeed need any proving, being unquestioned.

Let us consider, for example, the matter of Hunting, with which I propose more especially to deal. There was in England, in the eighteenth century, a Marchioness of Salisbury who kept and followed the Hertfordshire Hounds; in Ireland, at about the same period, there was a Countess of Bandon of high renown as a rider. In literature there was " Diana Vernon," who is spoken of with awe as having " guided her horse with the most admirable address and presence of mind," and even " cleared an obstruction composed of forest timber at a flying leap." Later, Surtees, and Whyte Melville, and John Leech evolved between them a few beings who qualified their prowess in floating over five-barred gates by suitable attacks

228

of faintness during emotional crises; but these were all exceptions. In other sports—shooting, rowing, boat-sailing—the rule required no proving, which was fortunate, as I think there were no exceptions. In art, a tepid water-colour or so was tolerated; elegant volumes of " Keepsakes " received the over-flowings of the feminine literary fount in contributions that ran smoothly in the twin channels of knightly heroism and female fidelity, varied perhaps by a dirge for a departed ring-dove or a sob for a faded rosebud.

Even in philanthropy, in whose domain the conventional Ministering Angel might have been assigned a place, " The Woman " was assured that she had none. I have been privileged to meet one of Miss Florence Nightingale's contemporaries and acquaintances, an old lady of over ninety, with whom to speak was as though one had leaped backwards through the rushing years and landed in a peaceful backwater of earliest Victorian times.

" Florence Nightingale ? " said this little old lady, buried in a big chair, looking like a tiny, shrivelled white mouse with bright blue eyes and grey mittens. " Ah ! yes, I knew her well. A beautiful woman, my dear; but she had that curious fancy for washing dirty men ! "—which, no doubt, expressed a very general view of the life-work of the Lady with the Lamp.

Probably when the history is written of how The Woman's place in the world came to include " All out-doors " (as they say in America), as well as what has been called in Ireland, " the work that is within," it will be acknowledged that sport, Lawn Tennis, Bicycling, and Hunting, played quite as potent a part as education in the emancipation that has culminated in the Representation of the

People Bill. The playing-fields of Eton did not as surely win Waterloo as the hunting-fields and lawn-tennis grounds of the kingdom won the vote for women.

In no region of sport has freedom " broadened down " with greater rapidity than in hunting. Of hunting, on the whole, it must be said that " Convention's casket holds her sacred things." The red-tape of tradition has long bound her hand and foot, until, say, the last five-and-twenty or thirty years, the proper place of woman in regard to the fox-hunter has been laid down in the verse of the old hunting-song—

> " The wife around her husband throws
>   Her arms to make him stay.
> ' My dear, it rains, it hails, it blows !
> My dear [*crescendo*], it rains, it *hails*, it BLOWS !
> You cannot hunt to-day, you cannot hunt to-day ! "

(wherein the wife, if right about the weather, was very probably right also about the hunting; and while, still in bed, she comfortably drinks her " early tea," the husband, with his collar up to his ears and his back to a hedge, is asking himself why he had been ass enough to think there was a fox above ground on such a morning. This, however, is not the point, which is sufficiently obvious).

It was pretty late in the nineteenth century, taking the unerring pages of *Punch* as a guide, before women were tolerated (later still before they were welcomed) in the hunting-field, a fact for which I find it hard to blame the then masters of the situation. In those early times women were obsessed (one gathers it again from *Punch*) with the need of making themselves agreeable, which frequently meant that they talked at the wrong moments and too much. (I am not saying that this practice is entirely a matter of the past.) If a woman's horse fell, she was probably more hurt than a man would be; in any case, her horse had to be caught, and some one had to mount her, which gave almost as much trouble as if she had been killed (I was going to have said without the attendant compensation, but refrain). Those early pictures set forth unsparingly the various feminine foibles. The lady who talks the fox back into covert, who holds up the hunt while she fumbles at a gate, whose horse invariably kicks hounds, or anything else that is near enough; even that unfortunate lady to whom a man has to devote his coat because her horse and habit skirt have followed the hounds without her. Improvement in these matters was gradual, but it came. The modern side-saddle did much; the introduction of safety-aprons did more, riding astride will probably do most of all. Di Vernon was, no doubt, seated on a species of howdah with a well-like centre, her right leg enclosed by two in-curving crutches, her left foot resting in a contrivance like a fossilised bedroom slipper. Miss Lucy Glitters and Kate Coventry wore habits that might, at a pinch, have enclosed a crinoline.

The safety-apron has possibly seen its most brilliant days, and the ride-astride outfit is fast superseding all others. Many, and beyond telling, are its advantages, yet, at the risk of incurring the contempt of those whose opinion counts for most, and is least worth having (I allude to the rising generation), I would like to say that the basis of good hands is a firm seat, and this, in conjunction with a ride-astride outfit, is unusual.

My own earliest recollection of hunting belongs to those pre-historic times when Man went forth to the chase, and Woman, at best, palpitated over her lord's prowess from the vantage-point of the family

outside-car, possibly even, if the day were inclement
and the scene the County Cork, from the purdah-like
depths of the family inside-car, or jingle. My first
remembered day with hounds was, however, a remarkable variant of the accepted rule, and is, for that
reason, worthy of record. A bagged fox was to be
" shaken," and to me, unworthy member of the
unworthier sex, befell the pony (whose age, sixteen,
just doubled mine), while my brother, of somewhat
tenderer years, it is true, drove to the meet upon
an outside car, in tears and a black spotted net veil.
The veil was enforced by the nursery authority, in
deference to a " stye " in his eye; the tears were
the natural result of this outrage upon masculine
dignity. It is recorded that the little boy, still, like
a heroine of old romance, weeping and closely veiled,
held a corner of the bag during the ceremony of
releasing the fox from it, but this alleviation was
entirely outweighed by the fact that his sister, for
reasons not specially apparent, was subsequently
given the brush, and bore it back to the nursery in
offensive triumph.

It is because of its remarkable foreshadowing of
the future that the incident has been rescued from
oblivion. It is now the girl of the family who rides
to hounds, seriously and consistently, and, when her
brothers return for the Christmas holidays, gravely
debates with the groom as to whether the pony will
be " too much for the young gentlemen." It is
melancholy to relate that the young gentlemen are,
as often as not, singularly unselfish in the matter of
the pony, and are more especially so when a day's
shooting is the alternative. The heart of the Flapper
is as yet untainted by the rival attraction of the
gun, and, so remarkable has been the progress of
emancipation, I have even known of hunting govern-

esses who took the field with their charges, and were the envy and admiration of those parents not possessed of so undaunted a deputy.

I have seen an old book on hunting which, in advocating the presence of The Fair Sex at a meet, offered, apologetically, the reason that such an intrusion would enable them "to exhibit becoming costumes, and would fit them to talk agreeably and with intelligence to the gentlemen after dinner." That was in 1830, or thereabouts; nearly a century ago, and a century that has, perhaps, done more to turn the world upside down than any of its predecessors.

Inevitably, as one ponders upon the changed locale of "the woman's place," the stupendous revolution brought about by the War comes to mind. Sports, as sports, have temporarily gone under. The muscle, the nerve, the vitality that they bred in women have been applied in other spheres, and in many munition works and hospitals have proved their value.

Hunting, alone among sports, serves a positive national need. At the beginning of the War it is no exaggeration to say that the Hunts saved the situation as far as the cavalry was concerned, and the Army, while it demanded the men and horses that hunting had created, and by whom hunting lived, moved, and had its being, illogically insisted that hounds must be kept going and that cavalry remounts must not fail. Thus it came about that "the woman's place," as often as not, was, necessarily the stables, and lady-masters and lady-grooms laid the axe to the root of a long-cherished monopoly. Not one, but many Hunts must, during the bad years, have gone under, were it not that their Masters' wives and daughters, instead of throwing their arms round their men "to bid them stay," as laid down by the song, strengthened their hearts to go, and, without considering whether it rained, hailed, or blew, took over the hounds and what were left of the horses, and " carried on."

I have in mind a Hunt in an Irish county, in which, what time the bugle blew the advance, the Master " dug out " himself and such of his staff as were eligible, leaving the Hunt in the hands of his wife, uncertain of all things save the way his duty lay. His wife stood up to the situation, as a good sportswoman will. She " carried on," she even " carried the horn " and hunted the hounds herself, afraid of one thing only, that when the Master came home he would say that she had spoilt the hounds. (It may here be stated that no such calamity occurred; the end of the War found the morals of the pack unimpaired.)

Only such as battled through those first bad days can at all realise what was involved in the game of carrying on. The wearing strain of the commissariat alone, bad enough in pre-war days, was enough to overwhelm the novice. Flesh, meal, biscuits, having doubled in price, withdrew themselves from the public view, and waited, in cloistered calm, until dearth had prepared those that needed them for extortions such as exceeded their darkest anticipations. And this was not the only strain.

The popular view of fox-hunting, largely based on Christmas numbers and their like, is sometimes justified, and " the gay throng that goes laughing along," exclusively composed of young and beautiful riders and horses, a flawless pack of identical hounds, a fox who is shot from the covert as from a pop-gun at the psychological moment, have, no doubt, occasionally occurred—" the time and the place and the loved one all together," as it were. The usual hunting record is dedicated to success, the glories and ecstasies of fox-hunting need not here be sung.

I should like to write the story of a hunting day more typical of this past time of war, and to show faithfully, if faintly, what are some of the minor trials of a Deputy Master, and, as Ireland is best known to me, let that day be in Ireland. (There is no need to say that the facts apply to no special hunt, since, given the position, they are practically common to all.)

Our typical day for our typical Deputy begins, probably, at some eight of the clock, when a message, poisoning the first and most precious moments of the day, is delivered from the kennels, to say, idiomatically, that "it made a frost early in the night, but the thaw was begun, and will the hounds be to go out?"

Peace ceases for the Deputy Master. She puts on her dressing-gown and visits, with groanings, "the glass." It is falling, which probably means snow. An icy blast from an open window (windows should be sealed, she decides, in a north-westerly winter wind) suggests an impending blizzard. "Take not out your hounds on a windy day;" she remembers Beckford's counsel, and longs to have courage to obey him. But the meet is advertised. The conscience of a good young Deputy Master is a very tender thing; there is moreover something attractive in the knotted scourge and the hair shirt to the zealot.

"Tell him 'Yes, if the horses can travel,'" she says firmly.

She feels reasonably certain that there will be no hunting. The governess is away and the children have colds: she has Red Cross work to do, and her unanswered letters face her as Banquo's murdered line faced Macbeth. But advertised fixtures are solemn things, especially to a Deputy Master; she gloomily gets into her habit. The post is no later than was usual in those days of war; it arrives in time to embitter her last moments, already made poignant by demands and inquiries from all and sundry of those over whom she has been set in authority (a meaningless phrase, that should be directly reversed where the ruler of an Irish country establishment is concerned).

Motors, it is needless to say, do not at this period exist; and the meet is nine miles away. The Deputy Master meets the hounds and the elderly whipper-in at her own gate. Her mare is fresh, the road is slippery, the hounds are demonstrative in their affection. For a moment she confidently expects to find herself and the mare on their backs in the gutter. "Wilful," the spoilt puppy whom she herself had walked, having first, to the fury of the mare, clawed, with tom-cat-like mollrowings of affection, that lady's shining shoulder, then proceeds to get under her feet, to the acute peril of all concerned. A bitter north-west wind, snow-laden and fierce, fights every inch of advance along the road to the meet. Our Master's hands go dead; the hounds' jog, at which she must perforce travel, does not conduce to raising the temperature, and the mare's exuberance of spirits, which becomes more pronounced where the frost under the surface slime is most slippery, does not find a response in her rider's breast.

She arrives early at the meet, a bleak cross-roads near a long wood. The earth-stopper only is there, an old man, versed in guile, steeped in lies.

"Ere midnight I shut every hole o' them, my lady," he says. "Oh! divil a beetle could get in or out o' them!" And again: "Oh! full o' foxes it is! Didn't one whip seven laying pullets from me wife a' Sunday night?"

The Master ignores the conundrum; she sees, scudding towards her across the fields, two women, and knows too well their mission. (Have I said that she is also manager of the Fowl Fund? She is)—

and a good number of that ringing company of half-crowns with which she daily stuffs her hunting-purse have left it for ever, before the iniquities of the foxes are all recited and the Field arrives. The Field (that "glad throng that goes laughing along") consists of the Hon. Sec., who is a woman impervious to weather, faithful more than most, and a little boy on a bare-backed pony, who wears winkers that do not conceal the hatred for the hounds that gleams in his eyes.

"Take that pony out of that!" commands the Master.

The little boy obeys with *empressement*, but as he retires through the centre of the pack, the pony gets in at least one kick before it is too late.

"I believe Mrs. Dash is coming," says the Hon. Sec.; "I met her at the War-work, and she said if her horse wasn't wanted to plough—she's begun her extra tillage, you know—she was coming out. You might give her a little law, she's always rather late, and Hennessy told me he'd be out——" (Hennessy is a farmer, mildly sporting, and much courted in consequence by the Hon. Sec., with whom such birds are precious as they are rare.)

A hail-shower, which might have been fired by a machine-gun, comes swishing over the hills above the covert, and decides the question of further "law" for the always rather late Mrs. Dash, or even for the courted Hennessy. The Deputy Master, with lips stiff with cold, "touches" her horn (a recent and imperfectly acquired accomplishment) and elicits a note that is not specially cheering, being suggestive of an abortive attempt upon a pocket-handkerchief; it suffices, however, for the shivering hounds, and the "glad throng" moves on into the wood.

Too well, on such a day as this, does the Master know the ways of X—— Wood. Along a cart-track, deep in sticky black mire, she moves slowly, encouraging the hounds, who are invisible in the thick undergrowth of the wood. She is not well versed in "hound language," and trusts the Hon. Sec. is out of hearing, but she does her best to keep things lively, despite the *silence morne et vaste* of the hounds. The central ride accomplished, the narrow tracks, cut for woodcock-shooters through the close-growing, stunted myriads of oaks, hollies, and ashes, have to be dealt with. The sleet-showers have less power to harm, but the going is worse, and the peril from overhanging branches more acute. The earth-stopper materialises mysteriously at intervals, with specious encouragement.

"Thry south, Ma'am! Oh, surely he's in it! There's tin o' them in it! There was a woman picking sticks and didn't she say he faced herself and the little dog she had, to bite them!"

The Master tries south, also north, east, and west. The older and wiser hounds string out at her heels, along the narrow ride. They have ascertained that there are no foxes and no scent. They listen to the squeals of Wilful, who is now hunting rabbits, with expressions that would befit Elders of the Scotch Kirk were brawling to take place during service.

The Deputy Master is reasonably certain that the foxes have been "stopped in," still it is her duty to try out the wood and she does it. The younger hounds have followed Wilful to do evil, and are indemnifying themselves for the absence of scent and foxes by running rabbits at view. The Master rates them in vain. They know her best as an over-indulgent purveyor of biscuit and minor delicacies; the elderly whipper-in is far away, outside the covert, on the lee-side of a fence, cursing the weather, the earth-stopper, and the foxes, with the lurid misanthropy of a minor prophet.

SHE HAD PROMISED THE COOLADREEN PEOPLE TO DRAW ROUND THE LAKE

The wood and its surroundings have been " made good," and proved bad; the Master pushes her way out of it, through a screen of branches and briars, over a stony fence, flops into bog, struggles out, ascends to a commanding point of rock (in the eye of the wind and the teeth of the sleet) and begins to blow her hounds out of covert. She thinks yearningly of her letters, her armchair, her fire, of, in short— " Home ! The woman's place " ! But, as she says to herself, she promised the Cooladreen people to draw round the lake there, and there was talk of poisoning the foxes if they were neglected—and there was that awful hill, Drumlicky, she supposes she is bound to go on there, too, even though she knows only too well that there isn't " a grain o' scent," nor the ghost of a fox above ground.

Poor Deputy Masters, who had, added to their other trials, the certainty that not a few among the non-subscribers to the Hunt had encouraged themselves in that particular war economy with the assertion that " the hunting-field is *not* the Woman's Place " !

I am far from trying to imply that the Deputy was unhappy. Far otherwise; I believe she would tell you that her toil had its own compensations. I am also inclined to think that for those absent lads, whose bodies were in khaki in far-away places, while their hearts followed their well-beloved hounds through the well-remembered home country, the place of those women who abandoned " their proper place," and went to the kennels (if not to the dogs) to keep the hunts alive till the boys came home again, has not been so very far behind that high place of those other women whose more splendid part it was to seek and find the woman's place wherever their country needed their help, or suffering called for service.

STAGE IRISHMEN AND OTHERS

" LET me implore you to recall that hasty negative."
Thus does Kyrle Daly, second hero of *The Collegians*,
remonstrate with Anne Chute, when she, in equally
splendid periods, entreats him not to give way to
groundless expectations, adding that it was as impossible that he and she should ever be united as if they
lived in separate planets.

A reader whose instructive privilege it has recently
been to study three volumes of the series entitled
" Every Irishman's Library," namely, Carleton's
Stories of Irish Life, Gerald Griffin's *The Collegians*,
and *Selections from the Works of Maria Edgeworth*,
is compelled to admit that the interval between
separate planets is not greater than is the interval
between this present-day Ireland of 1920 and that of
Carleton and Griffin. After a conscientious assimila-
tion of the *Stories of Irish Life* and of *The Collegians*,
a literary digestion of the modern kind, weakly and
pampered, is aware of such a stupor as is often
associated with Sunday afternoon and an undue indulgence in roast beef. It is a usual convention to
say that one " rises " from the study of a book.
The conscientious reader of either of these volumes,
classics though they may be, will, more probably,
crawl away on all-fours—if, indeed, the power of
movement remains with him. The introductions will
scarcely have prepared him for the effort involved in
a word-by-word perusal of the works whose merits
they so authoritatively proclaim. Mr. Darrell Figgis,

in his preface to the first of these, makes, indeed, a concession to human weakness when he says of Carleton that "few writers more demand, or would better repay, a careful editing of his works." It would have been more merciful had Mr. Figgis himself performed this office rather more drastically, and (as, in a pleasing variety of metaphors, he remarks) "sifted the chaff from the grain," and thus permitted his author's "real athletic self" to be seen. It must be admitted that the task would be one that demanded no mean share of intrepidity. It is a difficult point to decide if a peasant dialect, offered, as in these books, by the hogshead, is more tedious to the foreigner or to the compatriot of the peasant. The foreigner flounders on from page to page, seeking rest and finding none, accepting, with humility born of ignorance, the floods of elisions, of misplaced vowels, of supernumerary h's, that weary the conscientious reader without succeeding in bringing to him "the scent of the hay across the footlights." The compatriot, approaching the task from a different angle, asks himself in bewilderment if these extravagances and violences, these (to an Irishman) humiliatingly exaggerated buffooneries, convey any genuine suggestion of the Irish farmers and workmen who, with decent self-respect and sobriety, now walk this lower earth.

If there be a quality that more especially marks the recitals of a Southern or Western Irish peasant, it is a species of reticence, of sardonic under-statement, of intensity, indeed, but intensity implied and withheld. Their stories have something of the pregnant simplicity of Old Testament narrative. There is the same confidence in the intelligence of the hearer, the same unerring selection of the structural facts of the case.

It fell once to the lot of the writer to receive from a carpenter of Munster a *récit intime* of an incident in

his professional career, and its inclusion here may be
pardoned on the plea that, in some degree, it illus-
trates this point. The carpenter was a person devoid
of conscience as an artist, his main preoccupation
being to persuade his employers that things, as Long-
fellow remarks, are not what they seem. He was,
withal, an agreeable and skilled conversationalist. " I
was hanging a gate one time for Mr. C.," he began,
artlessly. " I had it hung when he comes to look
at it. 'Have ye it plumbed?' says he. ' I have,
sir,' says I; and that was a lie for me." Here a
hint of a pause, to make sure of the listener's appreciation of the position. "'Where's your plumb-line?'
says he. ' At home, sir,' says I (but sure, I had ne'er
a plumb-line)." Another pause. " Well, the next
day himself and Mrs. C. comes to look at the gate.
He asks me again for my plumb-line. ' Never mind,
sure *I'll* plumb it ! ' says Mrs. C. ' Have ye a bit o'
string ? ' ' I have not, Ma'am,' says I. Pad Leary
was there, and with that he said he'd give her the
lace out of his boot. I wisht Pad Leary was dead
and buried. She tied a light stone in the lace, and
she plumbed the gate." The quiet voice ceased for
an instant, while the inwardness of the situation
sank in.

" It was plumb."

The climax came without so much as a mark of
admiration to emphasise it. The artist moved on,
without comment, save that implied in the steady
eye that held the hearer's. " And faith," he added,
without triumph, as it were irrelevantly, " Pad Leary
had to walk to town for himself the next day, to buy
a boot-lace."

One searches in vain among the *Traits and Stories
of Irish Life* for any touch of calm, for any recognition of the preciousness of under-statement. Take,
in further exemplification of these great qualities, the

case of a recipient of Unemployed Benefit who recently presented himself with a heavily battered countenance at the bureau appointed to dispense this tribute from a grateful nation. "What happened to you?" it was asked of him. "I went to D—— looking for work, and praying to God I wouldn't get it," returned the petitioner smoothly, "and I didn't either."

Carleton's peasants, with their shillelahs flourishing round their caubeens, their preposterous courtships, their oaths with grotesque reservations against liquor, faithfully adhered to until the convert dies of delirium tremens; their faction fights, in which the combatants, with "powerful blows" upon the ear, "send each other to the ground with amazing force," and lie there, "the blood spurting from their mouths and nostrils," their legs "kicking convulsively." After which, instead of being, as the reader might justly expect, conveyed to the mortuary chapel, they spring again to their feet, and the contest is resumed with undiscouraged zest and vigour.

Mr. Figgis complains that it was not permitted to Carleton " to express a nation's whole and complete historic idiom." It is a little difficult to understand what is meant. Completeness in farce or in tragedy could hardly go farther; and if Ireland can accuse one writer more than another of having introduced to the world that wearisome effort of fancy, the Stage Irishman, it is indisputable that one of the chief of his sponsors is the creator of Phelim O'Toole.

"Phelim wore his hat on one side, with a knowing but careless air; he carried his cudgel with a good-humoured, dashing spirit, precisely in accordance with the character of a man who did not care a *traneen* whether he drank with you as a friend, or fought with you as a foe. . . . The droop in his eye was a standing wink at the girls; and when he sang his funny songs, with what practised ease he gave the darlings a roguish chuck under the chin! 'Why, faix!' as the fair ones often said of him, 'before Phelim speaks at all, one laughs at what he says!'"

An observation ingeniously introduced to show the entire competence of the fair ones to take their places beside Phelim as Stage Colleens.

The only date supplied in the introduction is that of Carleton's birth, 1794; it may, however, be assumed that about a century has gone by since these stories were first published. The Stage Irishman, as promulgated by Carleton, has expired, his great-grandsons in 1920 are grave and gloomy gentlemen, who talk sombrely of revolutions and find their pastime in republics instead of in " pubs." We have not, we humbly thank Heaven, to occupy ourselves with such high themes, and may now turn our attention to Gerald Griffin. He, in his younger and unregenerate days, raised, it is true, a stalwart company of successors to the heroes of Carleton; yet the fact emerges that the country people in *The Collegians* have a *vraisemblance* that, as it seems to us, is denied to the beings who storm and yell through the pages of Carleton. And yet, singularly enough, Carleton was himself a peasant, while Gerald Griffin, as we gather from Mr. Colum's interesting memoir, came of a family of good standing and education, and seems to have spent a considerable part of his short life in London.

It may be that, in Carleton's case, his very familiarity with the everyday speech of the peasant persuaded him that it was necessary to lay on the local colour with a palette-knife in order to produce an effect. Unfortunately, that colour was acquired by him—so we learn from the introduction—in parts of Ireland where an alien civilisation had, even in Carleton's day, vulgarised and coarsened what Dr.

Joyce has called the Anglo-Irish tongue. A hundred
years ago the familiar speech of the poor people in the
South and West of Ireland was Irish, but in Ulster,
and in the counties of the Pale, Scotch and English
settlers of the lower class had long since hybridised
the vocabulary, and vulgarisms that are easily recog-

" I'M AS GAY AS GARRICK ! "

nised as imported make Carleton's dialect distasteful
to a Southern or Western ear. In the greater part
of Munster and Connaught, on the contrary, the people
learnt their English from the gentry. The elegance
of a culture now outworn in the class in which it
originated still refines the Anglo-Irish speech of the
South and West. No self-respecting Southern Irish
peasant will admit that the weather, however fiercely

hot it may be, is anything but "warm." A wife accuses an angry husband of "unmannerliness before the gentry," and advises him, if he must indeed "loose his temper," that he should "ease it on the little boy when he'd be alone." If further proof of this contention is required, we may cite a saying of an ancient woman of Kerry, who, when questioned by her doctor as to her health and well-being, replied, "Thanks be to the merciful God and to your honour, I'm as gay as Garrick!" Where else in the three kingdoms has this phrase from the days of Dr. Johnson and Fanny Burney survived? It has the sparkle in it of diamond shoe-buckles, a whiff of scented powder clouds the air of the dark Kerry kitchen, where the pedigree of the aphorism is as little suspected as is that of the old Waterford glass jug that is on the dresser, "undher buttermilk!" These sayings, and many more like unto them, are legacies of the High Quality. The Munster peasant of seventy or eighty years ago had a vocabulary founded on direct translation from his own richly poetical tongue into the English that he learned from his masters and mistresses. A Kerry fisherman was asked if the sea were too rough for sailing. "There is a white blossom on the fisherman's garden," he replied. A poor woman, telling of the illness of one of her children, says, "It's quare now, I had ten o' them, but me heart's inside in this little one-een!" Yet another woman spoke of "the blaze of darkness" that painted the cheek of a fever patient. When these things are present in the mind, it is difficult to have patience with the storm of laboured facetiousness, extravagance and vulgarity that is offered by Carleton as the speech of the typical Irish peasant.

In *The Collegians* a different spirit is shown. The extravagances are reserved for the upper classes.

The peasants are treated with simplicity; their language is not devoid of dignity, even sometimes of poetry; their characters, with the inevitable exception of that of the heroine, are more truly felt. But it is impossible to believe that Anne Chute, Kyrle Daly, Hardress Cregan, can ever have drawn the breath of life. Young Mr. Hardress Cregan discusses with his college friend, young Mr. Kyrle Daly, "the polite world," and declares that—

" the customs of society appeared to wear a strangeness in my sight that made me a perfect and competent judge of their value. Their hollowness disquieted, and their insipidity provoked me. I could not join with any ease in the solemn folly of bows and becks and wreathed smiles that can be put on or off at pleasure."

To which young Mr. Kyrle Daly replies—

" My dear Hardress, if you were never to admit of ceremony as the deputy of natural and real feeling, what would become of the whole social system? How soon the mighty vessel would become a wreck! How silent would be the rich man's banquet! How solitary the great man's chambers! How few would bow before the Throne! How lonely and how desolate would be the temples of religion! "

" You are the more bitter satirist of the two! " says Hardress; which, in view of his own efforts, is a handsome acknowledgment. It was the convention of Griffin's period that the higher the birth the taller the talk; and to Eily O'Connor, in virtue of her exalted position as heroine, is permitted a similar resplendency of phrase. Eily, the peasant girl, runaway daughter of a ropemaker, overwhelmed by her own wrongdoings, but far from silenced by remorse, exclaims—

" Every movement that I make seems to bring down the anger of heaven, since I first thought of deceiving my father. . . ." " How will it be " (she asks), " if the boat breaks under us, and my father is told that his daughter was washed ashore a corpse, with a blot upon her name, and no one living that can clear it ? "

It is when we meet with Lowry Looby, with Poll Naughton, with Dalton, the dying huntsman, that it is possible to understand the attraction that Gerald Griffin still possesses for readers who are not too impatient of his moralities and conventionalities. Old Mihil, Eily's father, in spite of lapses into the purple that is usually reserved for his betters, can impart a feeling of pathos and sincerity. " I'm ashamed o' myself," he says, " to be always this way, like an owld woman, moaning and behoning among the neighbours, like an owld goose, that would be cackling afther the flock, or a fool of a little bird, whistling upon a bough of a summer evening, afther the nest is robbed." And Myles na Coppaleen, the mountaineer, with his " parcel o' little ponies not the height o' the chair," Foxy Dunat, the hair-cutter, " bowing and smiling, with a timid and conciliating air," Mrs. Frawley, the cook, and Nelly, the housemaid, all have that breath of life that is sought for in vain among the leading ladies and gentlemen; while Lowry Looby, with his songs and his ghost stories, is too good a character to be smothered and crushed into a corner by the solemnities of Kyrle Daly.

" And you wouldn't believe, now, Master Kyrle, that anything does be showin' itself at night at all ? Or used to be of owld ? " [asks Lowry of that unspeakable prig, his " young master."] " It must be very long since, Lowry " [condescends Master Kyrle]. " Why then, see this, sir, the whole country will tell

you, that after Mr. Chute died, the owld man of all,
Mr. Tom's father—you heerd of him ? " " I recollect
to have heard of a fat man, that——" " Fat ! "
exclaimed Lowry, in a voice of surprise, " you may
say fat ! There isn't that door on hinges that he'd
pass in, walkin' with a fair front, without he turned
sideways, or skamed in, one way or other ! "

Here is the authentic touch, and enchanting it is.
" Any way, fat or lain," goes on Lowry Looby, " he
was buried, an' all the world will tell you that he was
seen rising a fortnight afther by Dan Dawley, in the
shape of a drove o' young pigs." And Master Kyrle
simpers, " What a sharp eye he must have had,
Lowry, to recognise his master under such a disguise ! "
" Oyeh ! He knew well what was there. 'Tisn't the
first time with Dan Dawley seein' things o' the kind ! "
It would be both agreeable and easy to continue with
excerpts from the stories recounted by the admirable
Lowry, or to quote appreciatively the no less admirable Mrs. Frawley, Foxy Dunat, and Fighting Poll
(and it cannot be denied that the length of many of the
stories would make excerpts advisable); but possibly
enough has been said in support of the contention
that the peasants of Griffin are, on the whole, creatures
real enough to outweigh the artificiality of their
masters and mistresses, and to give the book a value,
as an historical document, that is at least as great as
is the value of its contribution to melodrama.

The temptation to turn aside for a few moments
from these three volumes to discuss other writers
of this period whose theme also is Ireland, must
not be yielded to; yet it may be said that, for
some dark and unfathomable reason, we find
in them all the same determination to extravagance, alike in dealing with the peasants and with
" the Quality." Lever and Lover raged along after

Carleton and Griffin—over the road that was, for
the aristocracy, a pavement of impossibly polished
marble and, for the baser sort, an equally impossible
bohireen. Even the sober and Saxon Anthony
Trollope was lured from the Close of Barchester to
batter over the *bohireens* of " Ballycloran " with
the MacDermots, and to deepen the conviction in the
mind of the public that Ireland was peopled with
Phelim O'Tooles and Lucius O'Triggers.

It is wondrously refreshing to turn to the cool
and temperate humour of Maria Edgeworth, and to
her style, in which the polish of the eighteenth century
gives brilliance to the presentation of a people who,
as Sir Walter Raleigh is quoted in the introduction
as saying, " had never before Miss Edgeworth's time
ventured to claim serious treatment at the hands of
writers of fiction." Selections from the works of an
author are possibly instructive, and are often beneficent
as a labour-saving device for the use of the unscrupu-
lous biographer or essayist. But if ever there were a
method of damning with faint praise, it is surely this.
Who, even in this twentieth century, would be satisfied
to take their knowledge of Sir Walter Scott's novels
from " selections " ? Miss Edgeworth, in her own
period and subject, stands alone, even as does Sir
Walter, in her determination to describe her fellow-
countrymen, " not," as Scott himself says, " by a
caricatured and exaggerated use of the national
dialect, but by their habits, manners, and feelings."
Miss Edgeworth's good breeding preserves her from
extravagance, her sense of humour saves her from the
ponderous sentimentalism of her day. The fact that
" Every Irishman's Library " is satisfied to offer to its
adherents an unabridged copy of *The Collegians,*
while it " selects " from Maria Edgeworth, seems
a matter for which Sir Malcolm Seton's apologetic

preface does not offer adequate excuses, instructive
and interesting though it is in other respects. It is
hard to understand, or to condone, the omission from
an Irishman's Library of a complete copy of one, at
least, of the novels that, as has been truly said,
" first gave to Ireland a recognised position in
literature, and opened up a new vein in fiction."

From the list of Miss Edgeworth's works, given at
the end of this volume of extracts from them, one
realises that her prentice hand was held tightly by
her father, and was early impelled to a dissertation
on Female Education. This was followed by the once
well-known series of stories for children, moral tales,
that, on one reader at least, had the unhappy effect
of enlisting all available sympathy on the side of the
villains of the piece. And then, astonishingly, came
that extraordinary *tour de force, Castle Rackrent.* The
more Thady Quirk's memoirs are studied, the more
remarkable as an achievement do they appear to
be. The book is in a class by itself in originality of
design, and—as far as any one save Thady Quirk
himself can judge—in successful realisation of point
of view. *Castle Rackrent* was published in the year
1800, and in treatment might have been written by
any realist of to-day. Its effortless composure, its
tranquil reliance on idiom and mental outlook, rather
than on mis-spelling and expletives, might have been a
lesson to its successors, had they had the intelligence
to perceive and the wisdom to accept the example it
offered. There is hardly a sentence that does not
betray a complete comprehension of character. The
main incidents, it is easy to believe, may, for all their
extravagance, have been drawn from life, the life of
that generation that riots through the pages of Sir
Jonah Barrington. What gives the book its unique

value is the power (that would seem to be accounted for only on the hypothesis of what is psychically known as possession) that has enabled a rigidly, frigidly brought up spinster gentlewoman to view, with the tolerant eyes of Thady Quirk, the blackguardisms of Sir Kit, the excesses of Sir Condy; to describe their drinking bouts, their matrimonial barbarisms, with just the admixture of indulgence and reprobation that such as Honest Thady would feel, and has inspired her to the supreme artistry of chronicling these tragical matters in precisely the jog-trot, unambitious, gossiping recital that realises for the reader Honest Thady, his pipe under his tooth, and his brogues in the turf ashes, as he sits in the corner of the big fireplace in the servants'-hall at Castle Rackrent. We can hear his pawky, peaceable brogue, as he tells of Sir Patrick O'Shaughlin, who, on coming into the Rackrent Estate, gave " the finest entertainment ever was heard of in the country; not a man could stand after supper but Sir Patrick himself, who could sit out the best man in Ireland, let alone the three kingdoms itself." Sir Murtagh, whose father's coffin, on its way to the graveyard, was seized for debt. " But," says Thady, " it was whispered (but none but the enemies of the family would believe it) that this was all a sham seizure to get quit of the debts, which Sir Murtagh had bound himself to pay in honour." Sir Kit, " who came amongst us, before I knew for the life of me whereabouts I was, in a gig or some of them things, with another spark along with him, and led horses, and servants, and dogs, and scarce a place to put any Christian of them into." And Sir Condy, who was ever Thady's white-headed boy, unfortunate Sir Condy, who, after his downfall, wishes to test the regard of his friends, and arranges a false funeral for himself, and a wake—" the heat and smoke and noise wonderful great "—during which the corpse comes near being smothered under the greatcoats of the *convives*, " that had been thrown all on top." So Sir Condy comes to life again, but " was rather upon the sad order in the midst of it all, not finding there had been such a great talk about himself after his death as he had expected to hear." Sir Condy dies in earnest of a Homeric draught of punch out of his father's " great horn."

" No," says he, " nothing will do me good no more," and he gave a terrible screech with the torture he was in—then again a minute's ease. " Brought to this by drink," says he, " where are all the friends ?— where's Judy ? Gone, hey ? Ay, Sir Condy has been a fool all his days ! " said he, and there was the last word he spoke, and died. He had but a very poor funeral after all.

There is a perfectness in this that is hard to match in any similar description. It exemplifies the ideal method of the artist, in music, in painting, in narrative. Touch and go. " He had but a very poor funeral after all."

TWO SUNDAY AFTERNOONS

I

It was Sunday afternoon, and the swards of St. Stephen's Green, Dublin, were blotted and littered with hot humanity. Peter Street, Patrick's Close, and the dingy labyrinth that lies between the two cathedrals, had sent forth contingents from their teeming population, leaving still an ample residue to fill the windows with lolling forms and jeering faces, as the churchgoers passed below. The soft grass of May was bruised by supine and graceless figures, unshaven cheeks were laid on it, and tobacco and whisky were breathed by sleeping lips into its mystery of youth and greenness. Above them the hawthorn trees trailed branches embroidered to the tip with cream and pink, children played shrilly about the fountains, with curses, laughter, tears and guile, happy beyond all comprehension, unhampered in their games by sense of honour, truth or cleanliness. The bells of trams made a ceaseless jangle along the sides of St. Stephen's Green, tame wildfowl on the lake uttered strange cries as family parties fed them with buns; everything human proclaimed that it was Sunday and that the weather was hot; the obviously divine grass and hawthorn said but one word, and that was " May."

At the head of the lake, where water sped and splashed down shelves of grey limestone, a quiet path wound among slopes and shrubberies; where it was most secluded a laburnum tree drooped above a bench, a golden and tasselled canopy for the loves of the gods, and now sheltering a stout young woman, with a large hat on the back of her head, and a brown fringe mingling with her thick eyebrows. Her dress proclaimed her the maid-of-all-work out for Sunday; the coarse colour that covered cheek and high cheek-bone spoke of youth and strength; her mouth was good-humoured, Irish, and vague. The blue eyes were well and darkly set, the slant of the eyebrows downwards to the snub nose might have been sinister, or might have been merely vulgar; the rest of the face gave the casting vote in the latter direction.

She was obviously one half of an assignation; the other half was already detaching himself from the crowd on the central walk, and turning into the path by the waterfall. He was a tall young man, shabbily dressed, with a heavy, pale moustache, and the pasty complexion that frequently accompanies the trade of house-painting. He came straight towards the girl with a laugh, and had her in his arms almost before he sank down on the bench beside her; the pert phrase of servants' slang died from her lips, and as he kissed her again and again her face flushed with the engrossment of passion, while his preserved the laugh with which he had approached.

" Steady now," she said incoherently. " Ah, steady, Joe ! "

He laughed again; a woman pushed a perambulator slowly by, children played in and out among the trees, yet the moments of greeting were not interrupted.

Few women can ignore, for any length of time, a hat slipping backward off the head; the girl sat violently up and straightened it.

" Well, ye got round the old one after all ? " he said, looking at her from under his thick lids, while she put a hairpin or two in her mouth and adjusted her hair.

Its strands were crisp and strong, and the gold sparkled in the brown.

" She was stiff enough about it," she said, replacing the hairpins and leaning back against his arm, " an' I towld her up to her face how I'd stop with no one that wouldn't give me every Sunday out. Little I'd think of walkin' away and leavin' her there, herself an' her lodgers ! " The encounter was reflected in the toss of her head and the thrust of her under-lip.

" What did she say when ye said ye wouldn't stop ? " asked her companion, disengaging his arm to light a pipe.

" She turned about as grand as ye please, and says she, goin' out the kitchen door, ' Ye can be talkin' to me about that to-morra,' says she. The owld fellow was drawin' the water for his drop o' punch, an' says he to her, ' Let Kate go out,' says he, ' I'll mind the door if you and the girls is goin' to church.' He does be good-natured that way."

" Doesn't he go out himself of a Sunday evening ? " The man was extracting a loose match from his pocket as he asked the question, and he asked it with indifference.

" Seldom, indeed," said the girl. " I declare ye wouldn't hardly know was he in or out, he's that quiet. He'd walk the stairs from the top of the house before he'd ring the bell, an' afther all I'd sooner answer the bell for him than another."

A pause followed, in which the pipe was lighted and Kate resumed her position inside her companion's arm.

" Well now, d'ye know what I think ? " he said—"that ye mightn't get another place so easy if ye left them McKenzies. By all ye say she's no worse than another, an' I tell you they're a queer old lot, some o' them lodgin'-house keepers. They're the sort that 'd run ye out into the street with the polis after ye if ye give

s

them any lip, or if "—he pressed her to his side
and kissed her—" they cot ye lettin' in a friend some
Sunday evening."

Kate's head remained on her companion's shoulder,
her heart was still beating heavily, and she looked out
from a delicious trance upon the sweet grass and the
embroidered hawthorn branches. How well it was
worth the hours last night when she stayed up to
finish turning her Sunday skirt, while her whole future
was bounded by the question whether she could get
out next day. After all, as Joe said, there might be
worse than Mrs. McKenzie. The girl at No. 16
only got one evening in the fortnight, and had all the
washing to do.

" Ye say she'll not give ye leave to go out next
Sunday? Well, supposing now if some one was to
drop round next Sunday evening when the family
was at church, they wouldn't find a new girl opening
the door ? "

" Well, maybe not," she replied, with the upward
look at him that is known to every nation and class
upon earth.

His arm came closer round her, and the present
moment rushed in upon her, shutting out past and
future. To the passer-by she was merely a clumsy girl,
with a large head, sprawling on the shoulder of a
dingy artisan, yet love and its dreadfulness were
there expressed, a fire struck from the heart of life,
to burn itself out in slow despairs, or mild regrets,
or in some sudden agony or extinction of death, such
as it is best not to foresee.

A clock intoned its tale of the four quarters, and
boomed forth the hours in a baritone as gloomy as
the bay of a bloodhound. Joe stretched himself and
got up; his face looked more pasty than ever as he
stood under the yellow cascade of laburnum.

" Come on now to Cooney's, and ye'll have a glass
o' wine," he said.

" Sure I'd be disgraced if I was seen goin' into a
public-house with the likes o' ye," she replied with
cumbersome coquettishness, her eyes still tender and
foolish as she raised them to his. " You know that I
never seen ye till ye gave me the time o' day a fortnight
ago by the canal ! "

" How bashful ye are ! " he retorted with a like
sarcasm. " Come on now, I have friends waiting
for me in it."

They walked away under the hawthorns, and passed
beds full of uniform battalions of tulips and hyacinths,
they crossed the bridge, with its grey stone parapet
polished black by an unflagging succession of boys
leaning over to spit into the water, they followed the
edge of the lake, with its hot glitter striking up on
their faces; her big feet hobbled on high heels, her
hat jerked with every step, she swung her umbrella
to imply fashionable ease.

Passing out of the Green near the Shelbourne Hotel,
they crossed over to Merrion Row, and traversing
that ignoble thoroughfare, turned at length into a
public-house near it. The swing doors with their
muffed glass banged behind them, and Kate found
herself in a semi-dark bar, with a crowd of men between
her and the counter. In deference to Sunday, the
shutters were up, and a ragged flare of gas combined
with the swing door to light the bar; there was a
babel of laughter, talk, and tipsy argument, the sour
smell of spilt drink contended with the weight of bad
tobacco smoke that hung in the air. Two men in
shirt sleeves were serving out liquor; as Kate made her
way behind Joe to the counter, she saw one of them
look at him as if he had been expected. He was a
small man, with brown eyes as bright as a bird's,

and Kate thought his pink cheeks and little black moustache singularly handsome.

" Is that yourself, Devine ? " he said, as he drove a corkscrew in. " You'll find a friend or two lookin' out for you in there," with a jerk of his head towards a partition.

Devine opened a door in the partition, and led the way into a little gas-lit room where there was just sufficient space for three benches round a table. Green and orange tea-boxes formed one side of the room, above them the sealed and serried mouths of bottles rose in tiers to the ceiling; the brawl of the outer shop came freely in over the top of the partition. A man and a woman were sitting at the table, with glasses before them; the woman's eyes gleamed darkly in the shadow cast by the brim of her hat, as she looked up at the newcomers.

" Well, Mr. Devine," she said in a twangy Irish-American accent, " you don't seem accustomed to keeping appointments much ! However, I suppose when there's a lady in the case we mustn't complain."

Kate blushed egregiously, and would have given worlds to utter her usual large kitchen laugh, but there was that about Mrs. Nolan's hat and cape that told her she was being introduced to high society, where gravity of manner befitted social junctures.

" Oh no, no complaints allowed here," replied Devine, with his arm round Kate, " not when I've brought a friend to introduce her to you, Mrs. Nolan."

Mrs. Nolan shook hands with Kate; the two men lifted their hats. It was an epoch-making moment in the social experiences of Kate Byrne.

During the next quarter of an hour other such were added, impressions whose vividness began to be clouded during the progress of a second glass of port. Her mouth seemed to herself to stretch into an unbroken grin, her shyness had vanished, she heard herself called "Miss Byrne" with a thrill hardly perceptible in the general affluence of dignity. Presently, in a manner not very clear to her, she and her friends emerged from the public-house; she leaned on Devine's arm and laughed a great deal, while the trams and the people in the street seemed pleasant, impossible creatures, somewhat top heavy, but full of genial intention. An outside car was standing at the edge of the pavement; they all got up, she with a festive shriek or two as her balance failed her; Devine sat beside her, and the little bay mare reached at her bit, and swung her carload away out of the rattle of the brown streets, out and out, by suburban terraces, and roads over-arched by trees, doing her work in singleness of heart, with keen and fleet stepping, with generous outlay of her powers, with everything that was a contrast to her vinous burden.

When Kate reached home her head was clear enough to remember at least one important fact, that on the following Sunday evening she would receive a visit from no less a personage than Mrs. Nolan.

II

Mr. McKenzie sat in an armchair by the lace curtains of his front parlour window, and looked out at the stream of life that went by him in Lower Mount Street. He was a small man, with pale eyes and a sandy-grey beard, and his Northern accent declared itself even in the clearing of his throat, as he sat, quiet and solitary, with his newspaper across his knee and his hands folded upon it. Except for the grey tabby kitten coiled on the sofa in decorous affectation of sleep, he was the only living creature in the tall and sombre house; the last of the season's lodgers had left a few days before, and his wife and daughters, gorgeously attired, had stepped into the last tram for Dalkey, with no intention of returning till 11 p.m.

The activity of the street seemed to make his loneliness more complete. Not a foot of all those that passed by paused at his door, every face was set on its own concerns, and whether in sadness or laughter, was a mere preoccupied profile to the isolated figure scarcely three yards away across the area rails. The paving-stones of the roadway were belaboured by big hoofs as the trams dragged load after load of human beings to the suburbs, bicyclists glided with their peculiar air of self-sufficiency, soldiers from Beggars' Bush Barracks swaggered in trim pairs and trios, children played clamorously about the dingy outlets of the lanes that debouch in Lower Mount Street. As an alternative to this outlook Mr. McKenzie could, when so disposed, study the contours of his back garden, a grey and airless pit, where a gravel walk afforded a promenade for cats round a bilious, variegated laurel and a sooty shrub of uncertain family. The vista was closed by a gloomy wall in which was a cobwebbed door, giving access to a stable, and behind all rose the vague, brawling voices of the lane that ran its evil course parallel with the street.

A stable and a coach-house were as superfluous to Mr. McKenzie as to the majority of his neighbours, and he had followed the universal fashion of letting them to a cabman and his family, by which device a comfortable sum is brought in yearly, and a rotation of epidemics is kept up in convenient proximity to the householder. Mr. McKenzie's eye, as it glanced occasionally through the back window, was expressive of the satisfaction that he felt at having, only the week before, made an arrangement of this kind, with a tenant who seemed anxious to meet his views in every respect, and a fortnight's rent in advance was at this moment locked up in Mr. McKenzie's cash-box. Mr. McKenzie's business transactions had always found their earthly close in this receptacle, from the days when it snapped its jaws upon the modest remuneration received by him for some minor position in the Custom House; and now it was scarcely to be supposed that he was entitled to much emolument for his duties of making out the lodger's bills in a copperplate hand and effacing himself and his dingy beard as completely as possible from their ken.

Out and away beyond the dripping locks of the canal that drives its way west among suburban streets, the sunset accomplished its slow and splendid perfection, undreamed of by Lower Mount Street. The wonder of light was perpetuated along that thoroughfare by the street lamps, flame blossom on rigid stalk, with the twilight falling hazy above them between the dusky lines of houses. A lamp outside Mr. McKenzie's window sent a square of light into the room, momently sharper and yellower as the summer evening darkened; as he lay back and dozed in his chair it fell on his face, with the shadow of the lace curtains moving upon his plain features like the mesh of a net.

Kate Byrne had lighted the gas in the hall and kitchen, and had twice been obliged to take the kettle " off the boil," before she heard the ring at the door that announced her guest.

Mrs. Nolan was dressed in black, with a large hat and a thickly spotted veil; it seemed remarkable to Kate, as she took her visitor downstairs, that so fashionable a person should wear tennis shoes, black canvas with india-rubber soles, such as can be bought for half-a-crown, but the magnitude of her own position as hostess blotted out minor considerations. She had, in honour of her guest, scrubbed the kitchen table to an almost unwholesome whiteness, black-leaded the range, and decorated the edges of the shelves with newspaper cut in a pattern; even the tabby kitten had not escaped the sweep of the broom, and had retired with the cold displeasure of its kind to the dining-room sofa, there to spend the afternoon among its bleakly buxom eminences of American leather. Mrs. McKenzie's best Britannia metal teapot lent its cloudy brilliance to the occasion, so also did various articles of wearing apparel, borrowed from the wardrobes of the Misses McKenzie, and disposed upon the person of Miss Byrne.

Mrs. Nolan was effusive in approbation of all things, spasmodically effusive, a more critical observer might have thought. She sat down and passed a handkerchief over her face, though the evening was cool, with the dust of coming rain rising before a rough breeze.

" Poor Devine ! " she said, swallowing a mouthful of tea with a gulp, " he was in a real way when he found he was ordered off for a week to paint the new hotel at Howth. He'd have been sure to come with me only for that."

" Oh, I'm sure ! " replied Kate in would-be sarcasm, her large cheek purpling, and her utterance cloaked by bread and butter.

" You mustn't treat that young man bad," went on Mrs. Nolan, her sunken black eyes taking in everything round her as she talked ; " I never saw him so fond of a girl, and I've known him years."

" Oh, indeed, I daresay he's been fond of plenty," said poor Kate, instantly tasting the bitter in the honey.

Mrs. Nolan looked at her with a strange, fixed

expression, the expression of an animal when its ears are laid back to listen.

" I've known plenty of women after Devine," she said, resuming the conversation with a jerk, " but that's a different affair. I can tell him that a smart, handsome-looking girl like yourself is the wife for him, and I guess I know what's what, after ten years in the States."

A gust of wind boomed in the chimney, and shook a door with a rattling latch somewhere in the back of the house. Mrs. Nolan's cup paused on its way to her lips, and was set down again quickly. She clenched the hand that held her handkerchief, and her full under-lip hung a little as her breath came short. Kate sat silent and half giddy with self-consciousness, waiting for Mrs. Nolan to continue. In the silence a whistle that might have come from the lane at tee back of the stable was audible, a peculiar whistle with two notes and a crescendo in it. Being accustomed to every variety of noise from that quarter, Kate did not notice it.

When Mrs. Nolan spoke, it was not on the topic that her companion expected.

" My husband has a notion of starting in the lodging business in this street," she said, speaking rather fast, " and I should like just to have a look round at the basement here, to see what sort of accommodation there is. I suppose that's the larder there," looking at a door with a key in the lock and a small square of perforated zinc let into the woodwork; " I'd like to see what sort of larders they have in these houses. Would you show it to me, like a good girl? "

She placed an affectionate arm round her friend, and walked her to the door. Kate turned the key and opened the door, revealing a gloomy interior of shelves decked with greasy relics of an early dinner.

" Indeed it's not all out as clean as I do mostly have it——" she began, and the next moment a dexterous shove thrust her inside the door, almost throwing her on her face. As she recovered herself she heard the key turn in the door, and it seemed, even to her untutored mind, that Mrs. Nolan had peculiar ideas in the matter of a practical joke. She, however, burst out laughing and called to her guest to release her. There was not a sound in response, except a soft hurrying of feet in the passage outside the kitchen.

" What the devil is she making a fool of me this way for?" Kate exclaimed, shaking the door.

She stopped to listen, and heard the door into the back garden open and close, and immediately after the kitchen staircase creaked as some one passed up it. Having again unsuccessfully called the facetious Mrs. Nolan, an idea occurred to her. The kitchen cleaver lay on a shelf, with it she ripped a corner of the sheet of zinc from its fastening, forced her arm through, got the tips of her fingers on the key, turned it with an effort, and walked out into the kitchen with a grin appropriate to Mrs. Nolan's strange outburst of humour.

Mrs. Nolan was not there, and as Kate stood in bewilderment, there came a muffled trampling of feet in the room overhead, heavy, confused, and yet strenuous. Her heart gave a thud, and she ran for the stairs with legs that were suddenly weak. From that moment fear fell upon her, ungoverned, and, as it seemed to her, paralysing, though her body was running at top speed to reach the hall door and escape from it. As she gained the hall there was a crash of falling furniture in the dining-room, and a shout for help that broke out half stifled, and was stifled again. From the open door of the dining-room Mr. McKenzie's struggling head and arms appeared, with blood running down from under his cuffs and over his fingers—Kate saw it as he clung to the door lintel—while hands snatched at his torn coat, at his arms, at his body. With smothered exclamations, with groaning and cracking of the strained door, he was overborne; he fell heavily outward across the hall with a man across his legs. Another man threw himself on him, and forcing his arms down, raised something that glittered sharp and slender in the gaslight, while the grey respectable head jerked and strove on the gaudy oilcloth.

With a shriek of " Joe," the arm with the knife was caught in the air, and Devine, braced to his one purpose, was thrown off his balance, and dragged from his prey. He was on his feet in a moment, and had Kate by the throat, trying to fling her back to the kitchen stairs, while Mr. McKenzie writhed and rolled in the grip of his other assailant.

" Joe ! " she gurgled out, " what are ye doing to him ? Oh, Joe, ye wouldn't hurt me——"

Her voice rose to a shriek as he flung her to and fro in the effort to throw her down the stairs. The reek of whisky was in his panting breath, and accustomed as she was to seeing men savagely drunk, men brutally rough, she could not believe his purpose, and clung, screaming, to the arm that flung her off. She felt his hand inside the collar of her dress, twisting it and dragging her towards him with his knuckles pressed into her throat. There was a feeling of suffocation, and she struggled desperately, until her senses began to fail, and the pulses of her head rustled and rung into numbness; there came in darkness a flame of agony in her side. After that she sank far and helpless in space, overborne by immense and crushing forces; then, in the stress, a final crisis and surrender.

III

Out of dark spaces of eternity there came at length a faint activity. Drifts of evil dreams passed by, like ghosts of things more evil than they; the deep-seated mind consciousness began to discern them, while yet the physical consciousness was far away. There were figures against light, with a blue fog round them; a long way off a voice said very lazily, and in time to a strange burring rhythm, " She's conscious."

Some one wiped her cheeks softly, tears were sliding down them, something was put into her mouth and she swallowed it; she coughed and the cough ended in a sharp cry that she herself hardly heard. There was a red-hot thrust in her side, far in, with all the horror of a pain never known before. She was in bed, and two men and a young woman were standing beside her; she thought that the girl must be a very smart servant to have her cap and apron so white, but as yet she wondered little at anything. It was a lofty room, with two other beds in it, both empty; the polished floor reflected the light, and a cool air came through a tall window. She did not know whether it were evening or morning.

" You're better now," said one of the men, a gentleman, she knew at once, though she saw things very indistinctly.

" Thank you, sir," she said, her voice seeming to herself heavy and lagging. She lay quiet, while a light hand felt her pulse, and the problem of whether it were evening or morning engrossed her brain. Fever drummed and rushed in her ears, her hands as they lay on the counterpane were remote from her and beyond her influence, her body was immovably bandaged, and all the while a cloud of uncomprehended catastrophe covered half her mind.

" I should say a few hours only," said the doctor who had felt her pulse, speaking in a low voice to two men at the door; " better take the deposition at once."

" The identification is the principal thing," said one of them, a man in a dark uniform frogged with braid.

" I suppose there is no doubt that it was not burglary ? " asked the doctor.

" No doubt at all."

" Then what ? Invincibles ? "

The man in uniform nodded. " McKenzie was employed at the Custom House at a time that some dynamite was seized there. He behaved very well indeed, and it was owing to his evidence that a brother of this Devine got penal servitude for life. McKenzie was looked after by us for a long time, till the whole thing blew over. It was worked up again lately, by a woman chiefly, supposed to have been in love with the brother. She has got away, but we shall get her in time. They did it very well, took the stable, so that they had command of the house."

" McKenzie had a wonderful escape," said the doctor; " he must have fought very pluckily to get off with two slight wounds."

" It was the girl saved his life, beyond a doubt. Her screams were heard in the street and made people hammer at the door. Our men made for the lane at once and caught these two escaping by the stable."

The murmur of voices droned inconsequently and laboriously in Kate's ear. Some one spoke close to her face, and she opened her eyes with a start. She slowly understood that she had been asked a question, a question about Mr. McKenzie. The blood rushed to her head, flushing all her face, but her memory could not drag itself to the explanation of the shock. Little was learned by the questions that followed; each drove heavily across her intelligence, and passed away into the deep oblivion beyond, though the instinct of respect for her superiors made her grope painfully to find replies. At one point she screamed out "Oh, he's killed! He's killed!" and fell into trembling and moaning; after this there was a pause, and she believed herself to be at work in Mr. McKenzie's kitchen, she was trying very slowly to lift a saucepan on to the range, but it was terribly heavy, and the effort hurt her side intolerably, and the heat of the fire was extraordinary.

Some one told her to look at something; she raised her stupefied eyes, and saw among quivering dots and rings of darkness her lover's face. It was pale as the faces of the dead, but the fear of death and not its serenity was in its tallowy whiteness, in its sick and desperate effort at unconcern. She felt her lips make an effort, and knew that she had said his name, whether aloud or whether far back in dreams she could not tell.

In the stillness that followed, the sound of a pen on paper was audible, then a voice said, very distinctly and slowly :—

"Is this the man who stabbed you?"

Her eyes had not left Devine's face; when the question was asked he lifted his and looked at her, as if his instinct told him that he could through them touch her dimmed perceptions, her dying heart. The blood mounted slowly to her white forehead, and everything around was suddenly very clear and loud and glaring; she saw the strange men by her bed, the well-starched apron and fresh complexion of the girl whom she took to be a servant, she smelled the strong air of morning that stung her nostrils strangely, and brought with it through the open windows the jangle of tram bells and the familiar cry of " Du-ublin Bay Her-rins ! "

She knew that fishwoman well, she had often bought herrings from her at Mr. McKenzie's hall door—Mr. McKenzie was very fond of a herring—she knew the way he liked them cooked, fried with onions. Her limp hands clutched the counterpane; that shrill and brazen call had joined her to yesterday.

" Is this the man who stabbed you ? "

It was the second time of asking. Her feverish blue eyes fastened on Devine, then passed from him to her questioners.

" No, sir," she said collectedly, " I didn't see him in it at all."

There was a slight movement among the onlookers. The perspiration broke palpably out on Devine's forehead ; he moistened his lips, and relaxed his attitude, with his hot eyes on the ground.

" Stop ! " said the doctor suddenly.

The nurse had her arm round Kate in a moment, holding her as she tried to struggle up in bed.

" Joe ! " she screamed, hoarse and delirious, " ye wouldn't kill him——" She strove with her weak, rough hands against doctor and nurse. " Oh, Joe, ye're killing me—oh, ye wouldn't ! " Her voice choked, and her head swung aside on to the nurse's arm. It had dropped scarcely less helplessly on Devine's shoulder a week ago, when the laburnum leaned overhead, and the sunshine struck the living sparkle in her brown hair.

The doctor made an unmistakable gesture to the others as they laid her down. The man with the writing materials closed his book.

MARTIN ROSS.

EXTRA-MUNDANE COMMUNICATIONS

To have the courage of one's opinions is a grace hardly come by, and often of uncertain advantage; in the present case it can only be hoped that some credit for, at least, this virtue may be bestowed, since it is more than possible that on all other counts approbation will be withheld, and it may be admitted that in approaching this most controversial of existing controversies, it is fully recognised that the lions in the path are many and fierce.

It is as singular as it is indisputable that, in a country in which a primary article of creed is an affirmation as to the Resurrection of the Dead, any effort to contribute evidence in support of the doctrine has the effect of creating an atmosphere in which discussion flames to flashpoint as soon as it is initiated, and what can only be described as a mediæval intensity of disapproval is immediately disclosed. Is it too much to ask for a reception of the question rather more modern than that accorded to Galileo?

It would be superfluous to attempt to give a detailed account of what is generally called Spiritualism, either historically, in its main outlines, or biographically, in an enumeration of the great names of those who have accepted the reality of its findings. These aspects have been dealt with by many writers of high authority and competence. A strictly personal and autobiographical point of view is all that can here be offered, whose only merit is its severe adherence to

272

truth, whose only excuse is the wish to acknowledge a faith and to express gratitude for a privilege.

I have personally been familiar with the amateur practice of Extra-mundane Communication since that now, alas! distant period when, my years being considered too tender for participation in such mysteries, I was summarily ejected from the room in which my mother and her brothers and sisters proposed to operate the Table. As far as I know, it was in this primitive manner only that they prosecuted their eager inquiries into the unknown. The table exists still, a light and graceful intermediary, with a single slender limb, finished with a species of elongated claw on which it twirled and spun. It was accustomed to follow—so I have been credibly assured—unaided, and with every token of affection that a table is able to exhibit, the cousin from whom the psychic power emanated; neither did it conceal its disapproval of those with whom it felt itself to be out of sympathy, and it would order their departure from the circle without compunction or hesitation. A very dictatorial little table, in fact, that ruled its gathering of highly self-assertive and argumentative persons with unvarying firmness. I believe that some statements, such as are now spoken of as " veridical " or " evidential," were received by this early group of inquirers, but I imagine that their methods lacked the sealing-wax and red-tape severity that would in these later days be exacted to compel credence for their successes.

Another group of my relations were also, at about this time, or a little later, occupied with similar experiments. I have often heard the story of one occurrence in connection with their circle that it is hard to explain on any hypothesis other than that which was accepted by those who were concerned with

T

it. It happened many years ago (whether in England, Scotland, or Ireland matters not), and but one of the " circle " now remains. I think I may tell the story.

A young man, personally known to some of the " sitters," had left his home, had disappeared; it was believed a love-affair had not prospered, and he had left the country. The Table had answered many idle questions, and another was offered to it :

" Where is ——? " The young man was named.

The answer came at once, startlingly : " Search the river ! "

Other details followed. It was said that there had been foul play; those to whom the facts were offered were sufficiently impressed by them to think it well to go farther with the matter. The river was searched —a swift, fierce stream, brooded over at the place indicated by the blind and dumb walls of a convent. There was no result. The Table was reproached with the failure, and responded : " Search the river again ! "

This time that which they were looking for was found, and it was evident that there had, indeed, been foul play. Nothing could be proved. Years afterwards a nun, on her death-bed, told how, on a moonlit night, she had seen a struggle and a body thrown into the river, but had held her peace, fearing publicity for herself, knowing that such evidence as she could give would avail nothing. One sees the tall, dark convent walls, well used to guarding secrets, with the deep river rushing under them, and can realise a little what was felt by that lonely, trembling creature, withdrawn from the world, and yet suddenly plunged into a sort of participation in its crimes, as she peered through the narrow window that should have been blinded, and saw the fight on the river-bank, and heard, perhaps, the splash that ended it.

" One of the nuns saw me," the Table had told, and had not been wrong in telling it.

Of my mother and her group of inquirers I can now recall but one instance of prowess which did indeed make a convert, but in itself, I fear, indicates the frivolity with which these light-hearted investigators approached their subject. A brother, just returned from London to far-western Cork, joined the circle, full of an intention—not uncommon in brothers—of proving his sisters in the wrong.

" I'll believe in it," he said, " if your spirits will tell me where I bought this pair of boots ! "

" Stafford ! " rapped out the Table, rocking in high excitement on its claw.

It had happened that the mail train to Holyhead had broken down at Stafford, and my uncle, souvenir-hunting we may presume, as well as killing time, had selected this eminently practical memento of the incident. Telepathy was not then the chosen shield and buckler of the disbeliever, and this scoffer of the eighteen-sixties jumped, Stafford boots and all, into the fold of Spiritualism, and remained there for the rest of his life, becoming, later, a member of the S.P.R., and seeing and hearing stronger and stranger confirmations of intercourse with another sphere than had been bestowed by the information as to the souvenirs from Stafford.

My mother had, I must acknowledge, a special *flair* for the occult.

" I am the most curious person in the world," she has declared, using the adjective in the sense of indicating a thirst for knowledge, and ignoring its other application. Nothing was less to her taste, or more serenely disregarded by her, than the orthodox disapproval of such practices that was more common then than now.

Thus it was that the idea of an indisputable force, unaccountable yet actual, grew up with me and my brothers, and any of those preliminary emotions of surprise, incredulity, or alarm that the practice of Spiritualism arouses in many did not come into the question with us. There came a time, when we were considered to have attained to years of discretion, when the family's interest in the subject was re-awakened by the enthusiasm of one of my uncles, a soldier of many battles, and one of the foremost of the fighters of the Indian Mutiny. It was discovered that one of my brothers and I possessed, jointly, the power of transmitting replies from the Unknown, in writing, to the questions which my uncle showered upon us.

I may admit that we were very unenthusiastic mediums. When one has but recently escaped from the trammels of the schoolroom, interest in problems touching the next world is negligible. My brother and I accepted the rôle suddenly thrust upon us of mouth-piece, or rather private secretaries, of the Oracle, with more reluctance than we ventured to exhibit. But at that period the young did, more or less, as they were bid. By means of our hands, messages and theories in response to my uncle's questions flowed in an abundant and fairly legible stream over sheet after sheet of foolscap paper, while the minds and tongues of the " mediums " were occupied with their own affairs, and took little heed of the out-pourings of an intelligence that announced itself as an ancestress, one Elizabeth Cockhill. Elizabeth claimed to have lived an earthly life in the Dublin of the seventeenth century, and soon became irreverently known to her descendants as Old Cocktail. I can now remember no very startling achievement on her part, but I can vouch for the fact that, whatever the force that produced these results, it was not due to intentional efforts on the part of its unwilling transmitters.

My uncle has gone on now to that sphere in which his interest was so intense. I hope that I shall some day know if he has been able to foregather with Elizabeth Cockhill, and has found out from her the particulars of the diamonds that she claimed to have hidden in a cellar in Dublin before her abrupt departure from this world—hurried thence, as she assured us, by the *Skean Dubh* of an Irish Rapparee. Following on these early efforts there came a long pause. My uncle, like his elder brother, became a member of the S.P.R., and soared to heights, or plunged into depths (whichever formula may be preferred) of experiment and investigation, and my brother's and my humble traffic with the unseen ceased.

It feels a far cry to the next world when one is twenty-one, or did so before the War changed all things, and the Old, who should have led, were left to strain their eyes after the Young, who had taken the lead from them and were shouldering past one another through St. Peter's gate, forcing an entrance, nor casting " one longing, ling'ring look behind." It is not strange that those who were left behind should reach after them, should implore for a word, for one brief message of assurance that those they loved still lived, that they were still themselves, faulty perhaps, and foolish often, but themselves; not glorified into remoteness or oblivion, into a state where, beyond these voices, these desolate earthly voices, there was peace. If that were to be so, then the Sadducees, who said that there was no resurrection of the dead, were right. One asks' not for news of the Blessed, casting down their golden crowns before the glassy sea, but only for one lightest whisper, one least sign that he who had gone over the Border was himself, that he had not forgotten, would not forget.

There are many things that do not admit, or are not capable of, exact proof. The certainty of the facts of any religion is one of them; the identity of the sender of any message is another. In these things, or rather in the acceptance of them, acts of faith are necessarily involved. One does not expect that the letter, signed with a friend's name, written in his handwriting, saturated with his personality, is a forgery, yet such forgeries have been successful. But is it possible to believe in a long succession of forgeries, of daily forgeries full of messages, of discussions, of suggestions, descriptions, and reminiscences, all steeped in the personal idiom of the writer, all instinct with the individuality of the friend who has gone away? There are very many such cases. It seems to me that accumulated testimony of this kind, though it may be, and generally is, incapable of absolute proof, gives a sense of certainty that cannot be shaken, even though its appeal is purely individual and is incapable of bringing conviction to the world at large. The personal equation comes in. The credibility of the witness has to be decided upon. He affirms, he knows, by a hundred tokens, that the letter is from his friend. Let the Counsel for the Prosecution shake him if he can. He may discredit him, but he cannot dethrone his inner conviction, and, after all, that is what mainly matters. Let us help the world as far as we may; if it will not accept our message, so much the worse for the world.

Probably very many of those who read this have proved for themselves all and more than has been said here, have known what it was to have found, in darkness, a beloved hand in theirs again, to have heard a voice that they had thought was for ever silent. But the school of Saint Thomas Didymus is a large one; its pupils are trained to face life and death without either faith or hope for themselves, and with very little charity for others. Stoically they accept for themselves the gospel of denial; they cloak their wounds, and, hobbling on, maimed and broken, retain no hope save that of kicking away the crutches that others have been given, and have received with so many grateful tears, with so ecstatic a gesture of relief.

But these are the people on the nearer side of the darkness. It may be asked what of those beyond it? As I write these words come back—

> " And if I die the first shall death then be
> A lampless watch-tower whence I see you weep? "

Is it possible that in the sufficiency of their happiness they have no thought left for those they left behind? It would seem that there are but two alternatives : either the creature who has left us is so changed in that supreme moment of transit that all he once loved has become nothing to him (in which case it is idle to talk of the Resurrection of the Dead, since the individuality, which is the most precious thing, has perished); or, if we believe that the human soul we knew is still existing, can we for an instant imagine that he is not—as we are—longing to call through the darkness, to say to those who are left behind : " Peace, it is I ! "

The writer has nothing to gain in urging this point of view—has, perhaps, something to lose, in asserting convictions that are still by very many able minds regarded with either pity or contempt; by others with horrified and indignant disapproval. There is, possibly, a good deal to be said for the doctrine of letting things alone, of not meddling with matters that are not understood. It is unnecessary to enumerate the many *clichés* devoted to this subject. It may be granted that it, like an unfinished painting, is best withheld from children and fools. It should certainly be entered upon with caution and with reverence. A paragraph written by Frederic Myers is in my mind, and I think that I may quote it, and, with the quotation, cease——

Not then, with tears and lamentations, should we think of the Blessed Dead. Rather should we rejoice with them in their enfranchisement, and know that they are still minded to keep us as sharers of their joy. Nay, it may be that our response, our devotion, is a needful element in their ascending joy.

E. Œ. SOMERVILLE.

PRINTED IN GREAT BRITAIN BY RICHARD CLAY & SONS, LIMITED,
BRUNSWICK ST., STAMFORD ST., S.E. 1, AND BUNGAY, SUFFOLK.

CPSIA information can be obtained at www.ICGtesting.com
Printed in the USA
BVOW04s1047120914

366585BV00030B/509/P